This book belongs to:

THE

_____

FAMILY

Date:

_____

Princess Marie-Chantal
of Greece

.. ..

MANNERS
BEGIN
at
BREAKFAST

Modern etiquette
for families

REVISED AND UPDATED EDITION

Foreword by Tory Burch
Introduction by Dr. Perri Klass

Illustrations by Nicholas Child

VENDOME

NEW YORK · LONDON

CONTENTS

Foreword
Tory Burch

I am delighted to introduce *Manners Begin at Breakfast.*

When Marie-Chantal mentioned she was writing a book about raising well-behaved children, my first thought was: perfect timing … Parents today face a unique set of issues—from iPhone etiquette to social media appropriateness and beyond. It's a new frontier. And there is no one better to weigh in than Marie-Chantal, a successful entrepreneur, and one of the best mothers I know.

Since the day we met, I have seen Marie-Chantal effortlessly navigate being an excellent mother and savvy businesswoman in both New York and London, all the while making sure her children developed into fantastic young adults with poise, personality, and—of course—impeccable manners. Even more than that, they reflect the rare values of their mom: character, integrity, and grace. She is clearly doing something right.

I first met Marie-Chantal in New York in the 1990s. As our friendship grew, I realized we had much in common, from our love of family to being working moms to understanding that raising children is a constant work in progress. My father had a wonderful expression that being a gentleman is not a part-time job—something I have often said to my boys. It is something Marie-Chantal also subscribes to—that manners should be a given.

I have always been a big believer in practicing what you preach, and Marie-Chantal is doing just that. Her elegance and strength is something we all can aspire to and I know there are invaluable lessons to be learned with her guidance.

This book is a modern blueprint to show you the way.

Tory Burch

Introduction

Dr. Perri Klass

The two most important jobs for parents are to keep their children safe and to teach them how to behave. This is true for all parents everywhere, in all social circles, and in all countries, and always has been. We have all lived through some pretty scary times in the recent past, with a global pandemic that affected every aspect of public and private life, including childbirth, work, school, social life, and family dynamics. Parents found that the job of keeping children safe involved new decisions and new trade-offs, and that the job of teaching them how to behave also involved new questions, new conversations, and even new technologies. But those are still the two basic parental assignments, and the levels of anxiety that many parents have experienced over the course of the pandemic remind us of just how seriously they take those jobs. Both jobs start out—when children are young—focused inside the family, with the parents at least partly in control; you keep a young child safe with car seats and vaccinations, with safe sleep surfaces and age-appropriate toys, by childproofing the house and feeding age-appropriate foods—but as the child gets older, safety becomes more and more about helping that child learn the skills to navigate out in the world, even if the world itself seems uncertain.

And similarly, you start out managing your child's behavior by patiently issuing regular reminders about saying "please" and "thank you," but your goal is a child who can go out into the world without you and reliably deal with all the situations that come up involving other people—from meeting them and eating with them, to attending a variety of events with them, to (eventually) working with them. The world is a complicated and uncertain place, of course, and nowadays we need to think about the virtual world as well—many things that children will do as they grow will have a virtual component, from Skyping with grandma to virtual learning, to social media with friends, to remote internships and jobs somewhere down the line.

The experience of the pandemic and the isolation that many people experienced have taught us all more intensely than ever that personal contact is essential and cannot be replaced—it's at the heart of child development, the heart of family life, the heart of being human. But we've also learned to take advantage of technology, and for many families, the rules around how to use that technology have changed—but so have the challenges. And as a parent, just as you want your children equipped to make good, sensible, safe decisions, you also want them to treat other people with care, courtesy, and consideration—in person and online.

These two overarching imperatives are also at the core of my own profession, pediatrics. It's our job as pediatricians to help you keep your children safe and healthy, and also to help you nurture their development and their learning. And since small children are always learning, every breakfast and every bedtime is a parental opportunity for teaching and for modeling, and a chance for children to practice new skills, from the fine motor function you need to manage your food to the art of making interesting conversation—and taking turns so you hear what other people have to say. That doesn't mean that you have to worry constantly about "teaching" them—they learn by doing, by watching, by imitating, and, above all, by interacting.

Manners matter

As a parent, helping your child grow up learning manners is probably your most important job after helping your child grow up safely and in good health. This is the way you help your child learn about relationships, with family members, with close friends, and with strangers. Consider basic family relationships: as a parent, you cannot (and should not) hope to teach a lesson like "Always love your brother." Frankly, life is complicated and families are intense, and your innermost feelings are your innermost feelings, and they aren't anyone else's business, as long as you keep them on the inside.

But it's completely reasonable for parents to set out the expectation that children will treat family members with basic courtesy. In other words, you can't (and shouldn't) enforce a rule like "You may never hate your brother, not even for a minute." The rule we can enforce is "You may never hit your brother, no matter how much you think he deserves it." (All of us with brothers—or sisters—will know that feeling.) In other words, you aren't trying to make rules about what your children think and feel—you're making rules about how they behave.

But the remarkable thing about learning manners is that how you behave does affect how you think and how you feel. A child who treats a brother—or a grandmother—with consistent courtesy is going to have a better chance of feeling genuinely fond, and of creating some happy memories together. Parents who focus on helping their children learn how to behave are actually helping them learn to manage their emotions, to organize their thinking, and to arrange the details of their lives.

Families matter

This book emphasizes the importance of family time, in a world in which (as pediatricians and parents know) it is endangered. Even as we accept that technology and virtual contact will play larger roles in our lives, we need to hold on to those real connections and interactions that shape children's brains and characters. It takes care and planning, nowadays, to make sure that family members face one another regularly around a table, and to make time and space for building the habits and rituals and silly family jokes that make up memories. Some of the suggestions in this book are about manners and traditions that have been around for a long time, but it's also about putting them into practice in the world we live in today, being careful and conscious of how we all handle the lure of the screens—which we have all come to rely on in so many ways, but which are also ready to lure our attention away from the real people around us.

Pediatricians try hard to give families good advice around screens and screen time, starting when children are very young (and we are still essentially saying there should be no screen time at all for infants and toddlers, except for video contact with distant family members). With such young children, this is a way of saying, over and over, that what matters most is real human contact and conversation; that's how they learn and how their brains grow.

Babies do not learn from screens and videos, they learn from interaction—from what is called serve and return, back and forth with another person. As children get older, we advise parents to set sensible limits, to be aware of what their kids are watching, and, above all, to watch with them, and again, build in relationships and interactions. And we know that, as kids grow up toward adolescence, questions of safety emerge, and parents need to stay in the conversation. For older kids, their health and their mental health may be affected in many ways by what happens on social media, and by their relationship with their phones, touching everything from whether they get enough sleep to how they feel about their friends. The question of when we do and don't look at our phones may start as a matter of manners, but it expands out to affect health and well-being. Pediatricians are going to be there, reminding parents to keep screens out of children's bedrooms, to put phones aside when it's time to sit down at the table, to know where their kids are going and what they're doing when they go online.

Pediatricians think about what's going into your child's mind, and also into your child's body—of course we advise families about nutrition, and we're big on healthy breakfasts and family dinners. So many aspects of children's well-being are bound up together in those family dinners; children's nutrition improves, and the risk of obesity drops. Paradoxically, during the pandemic, childhood obesity was a major issue—children were stuck at home, less likely to be outside, less likely to be getting exercise and playing sports, and many children (and adults!) ended up eating for comfort in a scary time. On the other hand, many families did find new routines of cooking and eating together, and there's a lot of potential to use those habits in helpful and healthy ways, going forward. Family meals, from breakfast to dinner, from the home front to the restaurant or the family trip, still remain a daily opportunity to greet the people you love, to eat with them, and to treat them well. The manners discussed in this book will take you through those family meals together, and also through those family trips, with attention to how children treat the people they know best—their own family—and also how they treat strangers in a country with different customs.

Manners matter

They matter for family life, which also matters for good health, physical and mental. Medical studies remind us of the merit of eating a healthy breakfast before you start the work of the school day, the value of family dinners, the importance of paying attention to how much time your children (and you!) are spending in front of screens. Above all, the research literature and the daily experience of every pediatrician reinforces the power of parental advice and guidance, and the surpassing importance of human interaction. We all know that we are working to prepare our children to navigate a complex and changing world; we want them to find it an absorbingly interesting place, and that we want them to steer safely but also find ways to learn from encounters with the many different people they will meet. We want them to be treated well, and that will depend on how they treat other people.

The great thing about family life is that you get to start over again every morning; we sometimes stumble and we sometimes squabble, but we always get that fresh start to try again. To say that manners begin at breakfast is to say that every day should begin with an effort to treat each other politely, and it's also to say that thinking about manners and behavior begins when children are very young, in the early morning of their lives, and that parents have the great joy and the great responsibility of being there from the beginning, to help them learn and grow.

Dr. Perri Klass

"EXCUSE ME, PLEASE."

Manners Begin at Breakfast

When the first edition of this book was being printed, I was caught up in the chaotic but extremely fun stage of strategizing its promotion. There was a launch party in the works and my schedule was packed with a series of book-related events. However, as I prepared to introduce my book to readers, life had other plans. The original version of *Manners Begin at Breakfast* was scheduled to be published on March 10th, 2020; the world was starting to shut down and the rules of etiquette were instantly transforming. I wondered what would happen with the book. Would anyone read it? Would it even matter? However, in the first few weeks of publication, I was pleasantly surprised to hear from readers who found the book helpful because it offered the etiquette rules for when one is sick. The book provided these parents with a guide to show their children how to sneeze and cough into their elbow, as well as initiating conversations around helping those who are in need. These were the topics that dominated our lives, and I was glad that people found the book helpful and that it resonated with them. I was also surprised by the book's success. Yet I also had to be honest with myself that, within weeks of publication, many elements of the book had become outdated. When my publishers reached out to say the book was going into its first reprint, we agreed that the text needed updating.

For instance, rules that I staunchly adhered to, like no screens at mealtimes, no longer applied, as I watched my sons eat lunch while they went to school on Zoom. There were many occasions when I brought my laptop to the kitchen table because we wanted the grandparents and other relatives to join us at mealtimes. The old rules of technology etiquette were morphing, and I had to readjust my house rules accordingly. Today, things are almost back to normal; so while there are new rules I believe are here to stay, we still have to remember—and incorporate—the old ones.

Truthfully, there's another reason I've decided to revise my etiquette guide. I'm at a new stage in my life. I'm actually tearing up as I write this, but I'm on the cusp of becoming an empty nester. As I watch my children graduate and head off on new educational and career adventures, I'm also beginning a new phase in life. Although I'm glad my children are all out in the world, I dearly miss the days of having a full house. Even though the walls of my home are adorned with photos of my family on vacations, at birthday parties and other celebrations, these photos make me nostalgic. I'm sure any parent who is still in the midst of school-run, homework, dinner, and bedtime battles must think I'm a bit batty in my yearning for such a stressful period in my life, but I do. Maybe one day they will too. Now, one of my most important goals is organizing time when my entire family can get together. When we do, I am in awe of how each child, nurtured in the same household, is so different.

What they do have in common is that they are all considerate. I'm not trying to boast about my children or my skills as a mother, but I do believe that bringing up your children to be respectful of others helps develop their empathetic skills. Also, as a mother of five, I know that each child comes into this world with a distinct personality, and each will require a different approach to teaching them good manners. However, no matter what that child's personality might be, we have to remind them that the world isn't just their own, and they must bear in mind the wants and needs of others and respect them.

We might not all share the same opinions, but we should be able to hear each other's views. Since I've graduated from parenting little kids, I can offer some useful insights into how to develop your children to become polite and empathetic individuals. This book isn't simply about how to dress for a formal party, or which spoon to use for dessert—it's about learning how to communicate with others. However, holding a knife and fork properly does matter.

Truthfully, my essential parenting goal was guided by the principle to help foster empathy. The rules of etiquette should never be associated with entitlement, or viewed as classist, but should be thought of as ways to raise children who know how to live comfortably in a caring community. Being polite and mannered means thinking about others. It means teaching children to share kindly and play respectfully.

Now that my children have grown, I will admit that the greatest compliment I ever receive is when people tell me that my children are well-mannered and respectful of others. This is my greatest joy. I've had many careers throughout my life, but being a mother is still the most important aspect of it, and I hope that you'll see this shine through as you read this book. *Manners Begin at Breakfast* is meant to help others remember to say "Please" and "Thank you" with meaning, which might seem like a simple concept but is incredibly hard to practice consistently.

So now I'll end by saying thank you for reading this book, and I hope you enjoy reading it with your children.

AT THE TABLE

"Family dinners are the one activity found to
foster the greatest child development."

— DEBORAH NORVILLE

Now more than ever, I see the importance of a family meal. This is where storytelling happens, and we learn about our children. Some of my fondest memories are of sitting around the kitchen table with my parents and siblings. The family table is a place where children develop not only healthy eating habits but also good manners and conversational skills. Carving out a few minutes each morning to have breakfast with your family creates a structure that is both nurturing and stabilizing. As I say, manners begin at breakfast.

Although I love to cook, I know it's unrealistic to prepare a home-cooked meal every night. And you don't have to serve a three-course feast; the mere act of eating together has been scientifically proven to promote greater happiness within the family unit, manage portion control, and possibly even boost grades. And when children help out in the kitchen, they learn how to set the table and work well with others. These simple activities can lay the foundation for their culinary and social skills later in life.

When your child is small is the best time to introduce a variety of foods and flavors. Be mindful of potential allergies, and take the opportunity to discover what they enjoy eating. Don't just feed them a singular item but present an array of different textures and tastes. Not only is this a proactive approach, but it helps fuel their willingness to try something new, while avoiding unnecessary fuss at the table when an unfamiliar ingredient is suddenly introduced.

Giving our children proper nutrients might be the primary function of breakfast, lunch, and dinner, but I think one of the most important aspects of a meal is family bonding. I believe that engaging in conversation is how we unite as a family. The family table is where stories are exchanged and where basic manners are learned. So, when to start and how? It should begin the moment you place your baby in a high chair. After all, as they grow, we give them utensils, tell them to sit up straight, and teach them when to say "Excuse me," "Please," and "Thank you."

As most family meals are casual affairs, we may not always follow the same rules we do when dining out with others. This doesn't mean that we should set these rules aside, of course; rather, we need a set of house rules, or guidelines. Here are a few that have worked for my family and some that I have gathered from my friends.

House Rules

Same time, same table

I love routines! Many parents allow their children to eat in front of the television or computer, or while playing a video game, as it may seem easier and we probably think that it makes the child happier. However, children who routinely have meals in front of the television or at different times from their parents don't get the chance to engage in conversation on an adult level.

Family conversations give your child a sense of belonging and help to raise children who feel comfortable around adults. The family table is where these social skills are cultivated, from holding a knife and fork properly, to engaging in meaningful conversation. It teaches children to be good listeners, which helps them to foster empathy. Encourage your children to join in the family conversation and to talk and to share news of their day at mealtimes; dining at the family table should be an enjoyable experience.

Children are confronted with change on a daily basis, which is essential for character development but can also be quite stressful. Establishing routines and traditions like eating together at a set time offers them what they need most: structure and a sense of stability. When my children were younger we served dinner at 6:00 p.m. every evening. Then it was bath time, followed by a story or finishing their homework before bed. Although we've now grown out of this family ritual, I've noticed how daily routines like this help to shape good mealtime habits.

TV dinner

Although dining in front of the TV is not to be encouraged
on a regular basis, it can be a fun way to bond as a family.
As an occasional treat, why not set up trays and watch
a movie with your children during dinner?

Everyone has a role

Just because I love to cook doesn't mean I want to set the table and clear
it every time we eat. So I enlist my children to help out. Giving children
tasks at mealtimes provides them with a sense of responsibility. Even placing
napkins or bringing cutlery from the kitchen drawer to the table involves
them in the dining process. Their responsibilities will then grow with
them. Eventually, they'll learn how to set the table, including the proper
placement of the knives, forks, and spoons, and take part in cooking or
preparing food—important life skills.

No phones at the table?

When I first wrote this book, I was a strict no-phone-policy parent. However,
as my children grew older, I slipped a bit and I don't regret
it. For instance, during breakfast I can often be
found reading the morning news on my iPad.
That said, I will select items from what I read
to initiate conversations about current events
with my children, as it's important they know
what is happening in the world around
them. However, as society becomes more
and more dependent on phones, I'm still
against bringing them out at the table.

I also worry that parents and children are treating phones as pacifiers, and it is true that a phone facilitates a totally silent engagement between an individual and a screen. In a group it creates a distraction, or an escape route, so that an individual does not commit in real time to initiating conversation with real people. Remind your children that, while the phone is here to stay, it must be put away at mealtimes.

In conversation

It's not unusual for people to interrupt one another during mealtime conversation. This was becoming a habit with my youngest, and when I asked him why he always interrupted, he thoughtfully admitted it was because it never seemed to be his turn to speak. This is all too common in a large family; often, the youngest's voice gets drowned out by the eldest's.

I believe everyone should have the chance to be heard at the table, so do encourage your children to participate. If one family member dominates the conversation, teach them the importance of listening and allowing everyone to have a voice. Similarly, if you happen to have a child who interrupts, tell them to wait their turn. Once they have waited patiently, be sure to give them time to speak.

"Excuse me, please?"

THE BASICS

Every family has its own set of rules, but there are also some basic rules that should be followed as standard. Let me give you some examples.

Obviously, it's unrealistic to expect your family to eat together every night, so feel free to tweak your family rules to suit your family's lifestyle. However, the basic rules should be your go-to guidelines for all meals, especially when dining with people outside the family.

By the time your child has graduated from using their hands to holding a spoon, then a knife and fork, they should have a basic comprehension of table etiquette. Bad habits must be corrected early! You don't want your child brandishing their cutlery incorrectly or eating with their hands. Utensil etiquette and good table manners can be learned—all it takes is a little practice. So let's go through all the basics that can be applied at every meal and also in everyday life.

Clean hands

Washing your hands before a meal is a simple task and a healthy habit. I remember my grandmother insisting on it when I was a child. Children are often a bit resistant to the idea, but try to get them into the habit of always washing up before dinner and coming to the table with clean hands. The bottom line is that it removes any germs from their little hands; after all, we want to pass only dishes around during mealtimes, not diseases!

Napkins

A napkin is a tool, just like a knife or fork, and should be used accordingly. Teach your child to place their napkin on their lap as soon as they are seated at the table, and to use it to clean their mouth—and never to use the sleeve of their shirt or their hand instead! It's also considered polite to fold your napkin at the end of a meal and place it neatly to the left of your plate, as it shows gratitude to whoever helps to clean up afterward.

My husband's grandmother on his maternal side had a lovely way with napkins. When her grandchildren arrived for a weeklong visit, they would find starched white linen napkins placed on their plates. Above their plates were the silver monogrammed napkin rings that she kept for each of them, brought out especially for these occasions. After their first lunch, they would have to roll the napkin up, place it in the napkin ring, and position it on the left-hand side of their place setting when they were finished. They would keep that napkin for the whole week. This concept is well suited to our eco-conscious world, so I urge you to give it a try; reusing a cloth napkin alleviates the need for disposable products.

Patience

Children should be taught to wait until everyone is seated at the table and has been served their food before they begin to eat. In most European countries it's common practice to wait for the host or head of the family to start; at the very least, a child should wait until a parent begins to eat before starting themselves. This may seem old-fashioned, but it shows respect. I always insist on my children waiting for an adult to start before they begin their meals. (Of course, this can be incredibly difficult when it comes to voracious teenagers, but I persist and ignore their complaints.)

Elbows off the table!

Little elbows (and any other body parts!) should stay off the table when eating. There's a saying I learned from a friend that's great for helping children remember to keep their elbows off the table: *Always, Sometimes, Never*. It worked with my kids—why not try it with yours?

ALWAYS

keep your hands in your lap

SOMETIMES

it's okay to lean your wrists against the table

NEVER

put your elbows on the table

How to hold cutlery

The only time a child should use their hands is when eating bread and other finger-friendly foods! Cutlery training should start early, when your little one is experimenting with finger food. As soon as they seem ready, introduce them to a baby spoon and fork. When my children were very young, I used to take little forks and spoons along to restaurants, and would ask for their food to be placed in a bowl, making it easier for their spoons to grab hold of the food. It's okay to insist on, and continually reinforce, manners while your child is eating. They might resist at the time, but they will thank you for it later.

Cutlery etiquette

American and European styles of using a knife and fork are quite different. I grew up using what Americans consider the European style of holding cutlery, but I was unaware that there were two versions. As I grew older, I discovered there are two distinct ways of holding cutlery. That said, there is a universally wrong way to hold it—never grasp any utensil with your fist and shovel food into your mouth. In addition, it is considered bad manners to tear into your food with your knife.

The American manner uses the knife only when a small morsel needs to be cut; once the piece of food has been cut, the knife is placed down on the plate and the fork is switched to the dominant hand to eat that mouthful.

PAUSED

FINISHED

In both the American and European manner, the fork is held in the left hand (at least to begin with), with the tines facing down. The index finger remains straight and is placed at the head of the fork, or just before the wider part, above the tines. The other fingers wrap around like a grip, with the thumb placed on the opposite side of the handle.

The knife is held in the right hand, again with the thumb and fingers gripping the handle and the index finger remaining straight, helping to guide the utensil. Don't place your finger too far below the blade part of the knife. The end of the handle should rest in the base of your palm.

Teach your children to cut food into small pieces using a back-and-forth motion, rather than tearing at their food with their knife. The plate should be kept tidy—don't let them chop everything up into a mess, ready to be shoveled in. And please—the knife should be used to push food onto the fork, not their fingers!

You should never use a spoon on its own unless it's for soup, ice cream, or a soft dessert. According to my mother-in-law, if you do use a spoon then a fork has to go along with it, as a friend. This is usually the case for dessert.

Utensils are also used to communicate when a meal is over, or if you are pausing during a meal (see above).

Soft-boiled egg-tiquette

Although there are a number of different ways to eat a soft-boiled egg,
there is one method that is considered to be correct etiquette.

POINTY
END UP

TAP KNIFE
HERE

*1. Place egg in egg cup
with the pointy
end upward.*

*2. Tap knife against side of egg
to make small incision about
half an inch down from top.*

*3. Cut smoothly through
incision and remove top of
egg completely.*

*4. Eat egg with teaspoon and/or toast
"soldiers" (strips of toast for dunking—
great for encouraging fussy eaters!) and
scoop out top of egg to enjoy on toast.*

KNIFE
TO SIT
ON SIDE
PLATE

Table settings

Knowing how to set a table correctly isn't difficult; the utensils, if properly placed, will tell you how to use them. Always start with the forks or knives placed on the outside of the setting, and work your way in after each course. Though children don't usually need to use all of the utensils that are provided at a formal table setting, teaching them the correct approach at an early age will ensure they're not fazed by such things later on.

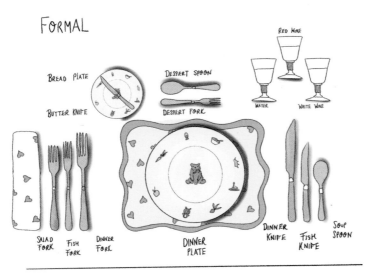

FORMAL

RED WINE

BREAD PLATE

DESSERT SPOON

DESSERT FORK

BUTTER KNIFE

WATER   WHITE WINE

SALAD FORK   FISH FORK   DINNER FORK   DINNER PLATE   DINNER KNIFE   FISH KNIFE   SOUP SPOON

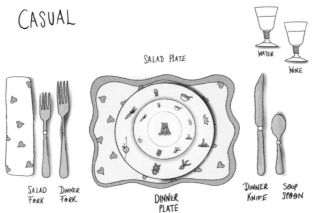

CASUAL

SALAD PLATE

WATER

WINE

SALAD FORK   DINNER FORK   DINNER PLATE   DINNER KNIFE   SOUP SPOON

Please and thank you

A simple "Excuse me," "Please," or "Thank you" goes a long way—in everyday life, as well as at the table. Teach your children to say "Excuse me" when entering a conversation during mealtimes (especially if they are prone to interrupting, as we touched on earlier), and to use "Please" and "Thank you" when being offered (or asking for) something at the table: "Would you like some broccoli?"—"Yes, please." "Please could you pass the broccoli?—Thank you." Be mindful not to say "Please" and "Thank you" repeatedly during a meal because when you say it too much, it loses its value. Being polite and demonstrating common courtesy at the table teaches children to show appreciation toward others, and will soon become second nature in all their day-to-day actions.

"COULD YOU PASS THE SALAD, PLEASE?"

Chewing

It goes without saying that children should always chew with their mouths closed and never speak with food in their mouths. Give them a friendly reminder, from time to time, to hold on to their thoughts until their food has been swallowed. Make sure they realize that eating with their mouth open simply isn't polite. If someone asks a child a question while they're eating, let the child know it's okay to continue chewing and to take their time before responding, rather than chew and cover their mouth with their hand. They can put their finger up to indicate that they need more time, and that they will respond when they're finished chewing.

Clearing up

When one of my children's friends dines at my house, I find it incredibly polite and it melts my heart if they ask to be excused from the table, or offer to bring their plate to the kitchen or to help clear up after the meal. It's a lovely gesture toward an adult, whatever your circumstances. In some cultures and settings, however, offering to help clean up could be seen as rude or unsophisticated, so always teach a child when it is and isn't appropriate. Everyone has their house rules, so stick to the rules and you can't go wrong. A good tip is to teach your children to observe what the children of the house are doing, so that they can follow their example. As a rule, when in very formal situations it's better not to offer, but in a casual home setting, an offer to help or a polite "May I be excused?" will generally be well received.

Dining at restaurants

Dining out at restaurants with young children can be daunting. No one likes to be seated next to loud, misbehaving kids, especially with parents who don't seem to have a care in the world. If you have set a precedent at home and family meals are a well-mannered affair, then you won't worry while dining out—right? So it's important to teach children the value of being respectful toward others while dining out, as well as during family mealtimes at home.

Always compliment your children on how well they are behaving. Whenever we went out to restaurants when my children were younger, I found it helpful to take crayons and paper along to keep them entertained. We also enjoyed playing a good card game, like Uno, while we waited for our food to arrive. It isn't impolite to bring useful tools like these out with you except at very formal occasions. Once my children reached their teens, we stopped drawing and playing cards at the table, because they were old enough to carry a mealtime conversation and didn't need distractions. Also it's rude for teens to be playing games at a table in a restaurant. But the no-phone policy still applies.

Breaking bread

When eating bread at the table (and especially when offered bread in a restaurant), never be tempted to cut it with a knife! Always break bread with your hands, then break it into smaller pieces, buttering each morsel as you eat it. (The only time a whole slice of bread should ever be buttered is when making a sandwich at home!)

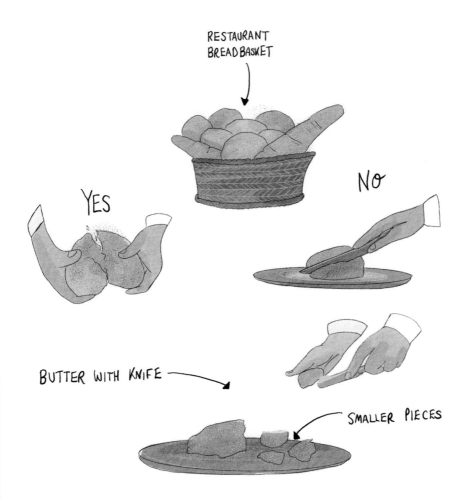

RESTAURANT
BREAD BASKET

YES

NO

BUTTER WITH KNIFE

SMALLER PIECES

Afternoon tea

When I was growing up in Hong Kong, on special occasions my mother
would take us to the Peninsula Hotel for afternoon tea. I rediscovered my
love of afternoon tea when I was visiting my husband's grandmother in
Denmark; she always served tea promptly at 4:00 p.m., and I knew that I
wanted to incorporate this tradition into my family life. However, when my
daughter, Olympia, was little, I would occasionally take her out to tea as a
treat. This was a childhood experience that must have resonated with her
because when she came back from college, the first thing she wanted to do
was have afternoon tea with me. This made me realize how important these
types of family traditions are, not only to us but also to our children.

This tradition is also an excellent way to prepare your child for how to
behave in a formal setting, since you follow similar rules of etiquette. When
I was little, my mother always reminded us to sit up straight and dressed
us in pretty dresses. I recall fondly how proud my mother was that we were
well-behaved at the table. I explained to my children that afternoon tea
wasn't like dining at a casual restaurant. There were gentle reminders that
we must speak in a soft voice, and there are certain rules one must follow
when engaging in this classic tradition, which I've outlined opposite.

Afternoon tea etiquette

Usually, afternoon tea takes place around 4:00 p.m. and one is served tea, along with finger sandwiches, scones, and pastries or cake.

Always start with the savory and move to the sweet. This means that you start with the tea sandwiches and end with the pastries.

Finger-sized tea sandwiches should always be eaten with your hands.

Scones should never be cut with a knife but broken delicately in half with your hands. Then use the knife to place the clotted cream, jam, or both onto the scone.

TOP TIPS

Should children order their own food in a restaurant?
Don't overwhelm your child with choices. Keep it simple and order food that will make them happy. Make it fun, so it's a positive experience.

What's the etiquette around food allergies?
If your child has an allergy be sure to alert any external hosts, be they parents or restaurants or catering staff.

Should you take your child out of a restaurant if they are misbehaving?
If your child won't settle down, taking them outside and calming them down before allowing them to go back in lets them understand that they were doing something wrong and need to be respectful of other diners.

What happens if a child hates the food they ordered or have been given at a dinner?
You should never complain about the food unless there is something wrong with it. You want your child to learn how to speak up for themselves if there's a legitimate issue, but to do it politely.

If your child keeps not putting their napkin on their lap or making eye contact at a meal, and you've pointed this behavior out multiple times, how do you address this without creating friction between you and your child?
Patience pays off. If a gentle reminder to look someone in the eye aggravates your child, you might consider distracting them. When Olympia was small and would get upset during a meal, I'd try to divert her attention, and ask her to help with the dishes. I recall her standing on a stool, happily enjoying having her hands covered in bubbles as she cleaned dishes, and a potential tantrum was avoided.

LET'S TALK ABOUT TECHNOLOGY

"With every word we utter, with every action we take,
we know our kids are watching us. We as parents are
their most important role models."

— MICHELLE OBAMA

Children today spend too much time on electronic devices. Truthfully I feel dated using the word *electronic* because, for me, it conjures up the image of a Walkman. As someone who embraces new technology, I see the impact it's having on children's manners. We are raising a generation who feel more comfortable staring at a screen than looking another person in the eye and having a good old-fashioned conversation.

This lack of human interaction is both unhealthy and heartbreaking. As the technological world evolves at a rapid pace, accepted rules of etiquette surrounding usage are, to a certain extent, yet to be established. My hope is that the guidelines I offer here set a good example for our children, and help them to lead a real life filled with human interaction, rather than a virtual one.

As I mentioned before, I love my electronics and get just as excited as my children do when a new game or gadget is released. I've been known to join my kids playing games and have worn virtual-reality goggles on more than one occasion. But even though I am intrigued by the digital world, I also understand that we need to set limits. These days, most adolescents have their own phone or tablet, and since these are portable items, they are going to be using them when they're on their own. This makes it doubly important to set rules at an early age, so that your child understands how to balance their technology consumption.

During the pandemic, students had to go to school remotely, spending excessive amounts of time staring at a screen. Thankfully, they're back in actual classrooms, but schools still use digital platforms, and many children must use computers for their homework and other school-related tasks. Schools also stress the importance of mastering computer skills and learning programming, but that doesn't mean that every interaction with a computer is educational. And, even if your child loves to code, you, as a parent, must find the right balance between screen time and real time. Easier said than done. It's therefore a good idea to lay down a few ground rules; here are some of mine, to help you get started with your own house list.

House Rules

LET'S TALK ABOUT TECHNOLOGY

No screens before bed

There are numerous studies stating that too much screen time before bed can prevent us from having a good night's sleep. When my kids were younger, my family shut off electronics an hour before bed, and this seemed to work well for us. One suggestion—although it might begin an argument!—would be to take your children's phones, computers, and tablets away from them at a set, previously agreed-upon hour. If you explain the reason behind it, they may be less reluctant to relinquish their devices; we all need our beauty sleep, after all, and they will get their treasured gadgets back in the morning.

I encouraged my children to read before bed, and when they were younger, I tried to read to them at night as often as I could. We chose books that would take a good six to twelve months to read together—the Harry Potter series, for example, and all the Roald Dahl books, and the complete *Chronicles of Narnia*. That way, we had set goals, and my husband and I would be sure to finish them. Reading to children creates healthy habits that can build their curiosity, boost memory, enrich their vocabulary, and help them settle down happily for bed, so if you can, make this a daily routine, allowing you to spend some quality time together.

Social media monitoring

I always kept an eye on my younger children's social media accounts. You might think you are too, but children can be sneaky when it comes to this new world, and many know how to create fake accounts to hide their social media presence from their parents! Talk to your child about what is and isn't appropriate to post on social media. You don't have to wait until the tween or teen years—start the discussion early.

It's up to the parent to decide at what age a child can open a social media account. I suggest putting it off for as long as possible! If you are getting pressure from your child to open an account or to get a smartphone, it's a good idea to raise the topic with the parents of your child's classmates and collectively make a decision. If all the parents adopt the same policy, you'll avoid the otherwise inevitable situation—and ensuing argument!—when your child comes home from school demanding a social media account or a phone at age eight because so-and-so has one.

When they were older, I let my children join some controlled social media sites, but I would always set the privacy settings to "Private," and make any other changes I deemed necessary. It's vital that parents continually monitor privacy settings as a matter of course.

While it's important to prepare our children for the real world, it's just as important to prepare them for the world online. Teach them about cyberbullying, emphasizing the need to think about how they communicate and to avoid hurting someone else's feelings. I always told my children to imagine what their grandmother would think before they posted anything.

This might seem a bit off topic, but it's relevant to today's discussion around social media and cyberbullying. I was bullied at boarding school. When you're bullied at boarding school, there's no respite from the bullying because you're at school 24/7. I bring this up because I see the similarities between this experience and the current landscape. There was a time when children were able to go home and get some relief from a schoolyard bully, but now there's no break for older children who have access to group chats, social media, and other digital platforms. Fortunately, for me, I was able to reach out to my parents and they promptly removed me from the school. If your child is being bullied, listen to what they have to say. To deal with this issue, show your child a world and life outside of technology. Try arranging playdates or get them to join a class or club outside of school where they might make new friends. So many children are so immersed in technology that they can't differentiate between the real world and the carefully curated one on social media.

Research has shown that spending too much time on social media contributes to childhood and teen anxiety and depression, so it really is a parent's responsibility to address this and monitor usage closely. Setting boundaries is a *good thing*. Children like to know that their parents care.

Gaming

As a mother of five, I knew more about gaming than I ever wanted to know. I tried to limit gaming time, but I also saw the value in it. In fact, for the past four years, one of my sons has played a weekly *FIFA* game with his cousin in California, and I love that this is the way they connect. Gaming also served as a social activity during quarantine when they played online multiplayer games together. However, these multiplayer games can allow interaction with strangers on public servers. I therefore only allowed my children to use a private server, I also insisted that they create avatars and never use their real names. Keeping your children safe and secure online is paramount. Another rule I set was limiting gaming to an hour a day. In addition, this hour wasn't a given, as the children weren't allowed to play until their homework and any required reading was completed; after that, they were much more appreciative of game playing as a bit of downtime.

Sharing

Having multiple children doesn't mean you have multiple gaming systems, tablets, and computers. Adults have a hard enough time waiting their turn, let alone kids, but we've all had to do it: think back to your childhood, when

there was only one phone line, for instance! In order to share an electronic device, the best thing to do is set a schedule together with your children (and do this at a time when they aren't itching to use it, otherwise there'll be trouble). Sit down and create a calendar that the kids can refer to, even when you're not there to enforce the rules. Learning to share is a valuable part of growing up, and a life skill they will thank you for later on.

"HELLO, MILLER RESIDENCE. BOB SPEAKING."

Tactfully dealing with a tech tantrum

Remember when your child had to give up the pacifier?
Electronic devices are just the same. Most of us have been guilty at some
time or another of giving our children a smartphone or tablet to distract
them while we take them on errands, to a restaurant—pretty much
everywhere. And then, when we take away the "pacifier," the children
are (unsurprisingly) enraged. So how do we deal with this?

When your child has a tantrum, it's essential to remain calm and
guide them through it. Tantrums are normal in a child's development,
and remember—they don't last forever. Once the tantrum is over,
have a gentle conversation with your child, and explain that they need
to learn to regain control of their calmer emotions. Although not
easy, a child has to learn to sit with themselves—to acknowledge their
feelings and manage them—and know that they won't always be instantly
gratified. Above all, be consistent and compassionate in your
approach, and don't give in.

THE BASICS

While every family has its own set of house rules (I have a friend who has a smartphone-free zone when she hosts playdates, for instance, insisting that parents contact her if they need to get in touch with their child), there are also basic rules that go beyond personal preference. These help to keep us mindful of both others and ourselves as we navigate this new technological world.

Since children learn from their parents' behavior, I have included guidelines for both child and parent below.

Smartphone/tablet usage

Etiquette for children

Whether you have a four-year-old watching a video on a tablet or a tween texting on a smartphone, as we touched on in Chapter 1, all electronics should be banned during mealtimes—plain and simple—especially if you're dining at a restaurant. Children need to learn that there are times in life when they will encounter more structured and formal situations. How will they cope if they're used to staring at a screen or playing a game during dinner? Get into the habit of reiterating the rules of behavior when they are out with their grandparents or in formal settings.

When a child is on a screen and is addressed by an adult or another child, it's important they know to look up and make eye contact when they respond. (There's nothing worse than being greeted with a monosyllabic reply and barely any discernible movement of the head!) Eye contact is an important social skill that children will carry with them into later life and that scientists have found to be crucial as part of a baby's development.

I know I'm not alone in worrying about the impact of too much screen time on children and the effect it will have on their social development; when I told people I was writing a book on manners, almost all of my friends said I must talk about technology and the etiquette around it. As mentioned earlier, these are rules that we are all still figuring out, but we do need to develop a consistent structure to follow.

For all electronic devices, it's imperative to create a rule about time limits. As this varies for each family, I would simply advise you to set a ground rule for smartphone and tablet usage and stick to it; even if it turns into a battle to begin with, eventually you and your child will embrace the routine and the boundaries it establishes.

Etiquette for parents

In essence: look at your child and not at your phone! This is harder than it sounds, especially in this day and age, when many of us receive work-related emails around the clock. As emails are often checked first thing in the morning, how best to manage the no-phone rule at breakfast, when both parents could be guilty of constantly breaking it? If you have to respond to a work email or text, excuse yourself and let your child know that the message is for work, and that, once it's done, you will be back at the table with your full attention. And remember: eye contact when you talk to them!

Social media posts

Etiquette for children

Eventually your child will ask permission to have a social media page. All children should have private social media pages, unless you've decided as a family to let your child have a public page. If you've been embarrassed by something your child posts, you are definitely not alone! As the parent, however, you have the right to make them take down the post. Don't forget the grandmother or grandfather rule we talked about earlier; it might make them think twice before they post.

Children's brains are, of course, still developing, and at times they won't make the best decisions, so if your child has posted something inappropriate, be sure to explain to them the reason why. Teach them that everything we share on the Internet is permanent and could one day end up in a public space (so if it's something they wouldn't be happy for anyone and everyone to see, they shouldn't post it). Again, this comes back to learning to treat others with kindness and respect—core values it pays to instill in your children at an early age.

Etiquette for parents

Social media can be addictive, and parents who post a lot set an example that their kids are likely to follow. When you're on a family vacation, pay attention to your use of social media; if you spend all your time posting pictures on your phone, your children will learn to place more value on curating a life to present to others rather than actually enjoying what's happening in the moment.

One golden rule is that parents must not post pictures of other people's children without permission. If I am ever tempted to post a picture from a friend's child's birthday party, for example, I always first ask if it's okay.

Text messages

Etiquette for children

If you have a tween or a teen, your child is probably already texting on a tablet, smartphone, or social media app, as most children are proficient at all these things. By the age of ten, they may be participating in group-text conversations, sometimes including a dozen kids or more. I always told my children not to use texting to say something they'd be afraid to say in person. I also made sure they were aware that texts, direct messages, and emails can be made into screenshots and passed along to others. Often this is done out of context, and it can be used to hurt another child's feelings. This is a good opportunity to teach children about a no-bullying house rule: in your family, no one is allowed to be mean to others.

No matter what their age, children should stop all communications via a smart device an hour or so before bedtime. (You may recall the switch-off rule I touched on earlier in the chapter.) And it should be a given that children shouldn't text at the movies, the theater, school events, family gatherings, religious services, or any place where they should be focusing their attention on something important or someone else.

Etiquette for parents

Again, if you have to reply to a text message while you are with your kids, excuse yourself, if you can, or let them know that you have to take an important call or reply to an email, and that, once you've finished, you will return your full attention to them. When you're out with your child or children, make sure you're not busy texting or on the phone while crossing the street or even while walking: the children should be your priority.

If you have older kids, text messages are a great way to keep a conversation open with them and to keep track of where they are and what they're up to. It's also a way of staying in touch, ensuring children and parents remain united. We have a large family scattered all over the world, and we're all on a family group chat. It's a wonderful way for the family to get together, even when we aren't physically all in the same place.

Emails
Etiquette for children

Emails should be considered more akin to letters than text messages, and greater care should be taken with spelling, grammar, and punctuation. Don't forget that emails are often used to correspond with teachers and school officials (and, in later life, employers), so it's worth instilling good habits in your children early on.

School-aged children usually receive an email address from their school, which they are expected to use for school correspondence. Emails should be written in a formal tone—for example:

Dear Mrs./Mr./Ms./Mx. [teacher's last name],

At the end of the email, they should sign it with:
Yours sincerely,
[with their full name]
or
Best,
[with their first name only]

Teachers will be on the lookout for any spelling errors, so be sure to remind your child to carefully check their email message twice before sending!

When it comes to addressing other adults, such as a friend's parent, this usually comes down to the adult's preference. (When I was a child it was "Mr. or Mrs. X," no question, but these days, adults may prefer to be addressed by their first name.) Once the adult has expressed their preference, your child should stick to it.

Again, as with text messages, it's important that children learn they shouldn't write anything in an email that they wouldn't say in person.

Etiquette for parents

Invitations for a playdate and party invitations can be sent via email. (Playdate invitations can also be sent via text message.) When sending an email to a group, be sure to send it as a blind carbon copy, as some people prefer to protect their privacy and don't want to share their email addresses with people they don't know. (Don't forget that sharing email recipients in effect means you are also sharing the party list, and not everyone may be included, so it's always best to keep it private.) If names are included in the email distribution, reply only to the host, or the appropriate person, not to the entire list (this can sometimes be tricky to negotiate when replying to an email thread). You should also reply in a timely fashion!

When corresponding with school officials such as a teacher, principal, or any important member of faculty in a school, always address them as "Dear Mr./Mrs./Ms./Mx. …" and when signing off, do the same, including your title and first and last name.

Top Tips

Can a parent post pictures from a birthday party on social media?

I always ask permission, as some parents do not want to have photos of their child shared on social media. Also be mindful that children who weren't invited might learn about the party from these posts.

Should my child have a YouTube account?

This is a personal decision, but YouTube is intended for children aged thirteen and over. If your child wants to create videos/movies on YouTube, make sure you monitor their account or create a private one.

My child was unfriended on Instagram. Do I reach out to the parent?

Talk to your child about it first, and then assess the situation. This could be a form of bullying and, if so, you might want to talk with the parent.

Should children allow kids they don't know to follow their social media account?

It's important to teach your children to be mindful of who is following them. Many children let friends of friends follow their accounts. It can be hard to know if all followers are legitimate, however, so review your children's social media contacts regularly.

I hosted a playdate and my daughter and her friend wanted to create a movie on her iPad. At what age should I let them navigate technology on their own? Or is it best to have a tech-free environment for a playdate?

If the movie is for social media, I would check what they are posting. Also, you might suggest the children spend half the playdate making the movie and the other half technology-free. It's challenging to host a tech-free playdate, but I do know people who have, and they survived!

TO WEAR *or* NOT TO WEAR

"Dressing well is a form of good manners."

— TOM FORD

When my daughter was young, she was very strong-willed. This was especially true when it came to choosing what she wanted to wear—which had to be a dress. At first, I would pick one and she seemed to be happy with my choice, but that phase ended quickly and it soon turned into a battle. She was only five years old at the time, and I grew frustrated as to how we would solve this ongoing morning issue. So one day, while we were at the pediatrician's office, I reached out to our trusted doctor, Dr. Davies, for advice. He suggested that I choose three dresses and, out of those three, she could pick one. He explained that if we continued to fight and I gave in, she would grow up never listening to rules. He also noted that if I always chose what she was to wear, it wouldn't be a healthy foundation for her self-esteem. He believed in compromises, and I've always loved his advice.

"DARLING, YOU MAY CHOOSE ON

In addition to the often stressful morning routine, where choosing an outfit can turn into a tantrum, there are other obstacles when it comes to children and clothes. We've all known a child who grows attached to a certain item of clothing that they want to wear every day, whether a beloved bathing suit or an old T-shirt. Then there are the children who like to wear costumes such as capes or other bizarre accessories at all times. I'm all for letting them explore, but there are times when structure and a dress code are both helpful and necessary. Just as you wouldn't send your child to gym class in formal shoes, neither should they go to school dressed as if they were going to the opera or a Halloween party! I'm not a psychologist, so I cannot offer advice on how to get your child to give up an item of clothing they feel very passionately about (if you reach an impasse, it might be worth seeking professional advice), but I can certainly go over the rules of etiquette that I believe to be helpful in dressing for various occasions.

Birthday parties, weddings, christenings, bar/bat/b'nai mitzvahs, holidays, formal and nonformal occasions ... These days, children are invited to events at just about any age, and their social calendar can fill up fast. I therefore find I am often asked what is and isn't appropriate for them to wear. But before we take a look at this, I must first cover my essential house rules about fashion and hygiene.

House Rules

Bathing

What your kids wear is important, but equally important is being clean. When you have little ones, bath time is the best way to help them wind down after a busy day. It also teaches them that cleanliness is integral to being neat and tidy in appearance, and provides a good routine to get them ready for bed. In addition, getting them into the habit early helps structure a discipline in hygiene and self-care that will serve them well in later years. As your children get older, they will become conscious of body odor and will understand the importance of bathing, but there is a long stretch when this isn't the case. My family rule was bath time every night, then off to bed for story time.

Make sure your children know how to use soap or body wash so that when they are older they will be able to wash independently. Tween boys may need a bit of extra encouragement to wash; if you meet resistance, stress that showers or baths can be short, but they must happen!

Grooming

While a child may shower every day, that doesn't necessarily mean they are entirely clean. There is nothing more off-putting than seeing a child with a dirty face or with dirt under their fingernails. I am a fan of the old-school yellow-duck scrubbing brush to clean glitter, soil, and everything else that gets caught under a child's fingernails. This can be done in the bath or at the sink. Keeping your child's nails cut short will also help to keep dirt to a minimum. Get them into the habit of washing their hands before and after meals and making sure their face is clean after eating.

Teeth must be brushed twice a day, upon waking and just before bed. If your child is a tween, they might want to put on deodorant; I tend to favor organic brands. Hair should always be clean and brushed. When we were little, my father would always send me or my sister away to brush our hair before we were allowed to sit at the table. In this day and age, it can be difficult to enforce the idea that children should "dress for dinner," but we can still embrace the idea that families should appear presentable when they eat together. No adult really wants to see (or smell!) an unkempt child at the dinner table, and getting your children to adopt hygienic habits early on will help them to fit in socially in later years and not run the risk of feeling excluded.

Clothes

When I was growing up, my mother told me to always dress nicely because you never know who you'll run into. Obviously, like every child, I immediately dismissed her advice. I will say that every time I walked out into the street looking not quite right, I would inevitably run into someone special. My mother was right! You never know who you will bump into, and you don't want to make a bad impression. I passed this advice along to my kids. This doesn't mean dressing to the nines every time you leave the house. My rules are simply that no matter what my children wear, their attire should be clean not stained, and pressed when in a formal situation. I expected my children to fold their clothes and keep their closets tidy.

When my kids were younger, if I felt an outfit was inappropriate, I would let them know and ask them to change. I didn't want to be a dictator, and I noticed that gentle guidance and an explanation helped. That aside, if you have a tween girl, you might be shocked at their fashion choices. Tween and teen girls today dress a bit differently than my generation did, and we have to respect their choices while also helping them to make wise ones. If your daughter is wearing a shirt that reveals her bare midriff, for example, you might want to suggest that she takes along a sweater, so she can cover up in certain situations. Of course, if you've ever walked past a group of middle-school girls, the fashion of the moment will be all too evident. Speaking from personal experience, suffice it to say there are likely to be battles ahead, and a healthy compromise is usually the best way to move forward.

Self-expression and socks with no holes!

I love children's fashion—so much so that I started my own children's clothing brand. In the last two decades, I have spent more time analyzing fashion trends than I'd like to admit. When my children were little, I liked them to be appropriately dressed, but I also admire a child who has a strong sense of self and wants to express themselves through their fashion choices. So why not let them have a little fun? That said, if your child looks disheveled, it's time to get involved and teach them how to make better choices. Socks should be be discarded or mended if they have holes, and clothes that have been outgrown should be donated to charity.

In a world where CEOs wear jeans as they deliver keynote speeches, we have entered a new reality of fashion rules. Even fashion brands create silk pajama sets to be worn out to dinner, and post-pandemic, some teens and tweens wear pajama pants or sweatpants to school. That said, trends come and go, and although the rules have also changed for kids, there are some that should still be followed. As a parent, these rules matter, because they give your child the tools to know how to dress appropriately for certain occasions, and these are invaluable skills that will help them in their adult lives.

On the following pages you will find the basic rules for dressing with style and grace to suit a variety of occasions.

Dressing etiquette: Gender considerations

While the following pages set out some of the traditional clothing guidelines for boys and girls, these days the boundaries are not always so clearly defined. If your child doesn't want to be pigeonholed into dressing one way or another, talk to them about what they would feel comfortable wearing. Agree on an outfit that still fits within the parameters required by the event—whether casual, informal, or formal—and take it from there. Of course, if there are no formalities to observe, then anything goes (within reason!).

While we all have to wear clothing that may not be our first choice from time to time, no one should ever be forced to wear something that they feel doesn't reflect who they are.

What to wear to the park

There is no need to destroy a nice outfit for a trip to the park or playground. Dress your child in something they feel comfortable in and won't mind ripping or getting dirty. A T-shirt, shorts, sweatpants, and other casual clothes are appropriate for this kind of outing.

What to wear to a restaurant

Obviously, if you're dining out at a fast-food or casual restaurant, you don't need formal attire. However, if you're dining somewhere a little fancier, a boy should wear something like a collared polo, slacks, and sneakers. A girl can wear a dress, a skirt, or pants, and a sweater or a nice hoodie top and a collared shirt.

What to wear to a party

This depends on the type of party. Dress your child appropriately for the event—it can be fun and sparkly too. If it's a party at a kid's venue with an activity, dress them in something suited to the activity that they can also wear for the duration of the party. If it's an outdoor event, they might want to dress as if they were going to a park. If the party is at someone's house and is a bit more formal, dress your child in clothes that they would wear when dining out at a nice restaurant (see opposite).

INFORMAL　　FORMAL　　BLACK TIE

What to wear to a formal party

Boys should wear a button-down shirt, a tie, a jacket, and slacks. They don't necessarily have to wear formal shoes, but they can do so if you have a pair at hand—though make sure they are polished! When my boys were younger, I encouraged them to dress formally but with a fun element, like some nice Converse sneakers with their suits. That way, I wasn't being too strict. The trick is to let them choose but teach them the dress codes. For girls, a dress is usually appropriate, but if your daughter wants to wear pants or shorts then be sure to smarten them up. A skirt is also an easy option with a pretty top or sweater. Remember: formal means you need to make an effort.

TIE
"IF APPROPRIATE"

What to wear to a formal dinner

At a formal event, a boy should wear a white, pale blue, checked, or striped button-down shirt, with suit pants or chinos, and a jacket. They can wear either a black or brown belt, though brown is usually considered more casual. For girls, dresses are appropriate, and make it fun.

Top Tips

How often should a child get their hair cut?

When my son was in school in the UK, they had strict rules about hair. It couldn't be longer than two fingers below the ear—which got me into trouble as I was styling his hair in a surfer cut at the time. If you want to keep your son's hair short, get it trimmed around every six weeks, though obviously it will depend on how fast his hair grows. Girls should get their hair trimmed once every six to eight weeks. There is no rule here, and parents should make the decision together with their kids, but, as with all things, the principles you establish will set the discipline that will help them manage later in life.

Is it okay to let your child leave the house in pajamas?

Although this is a growing fashion trend, especially among grown-ups, I don't feel it's polite to wear your real pajamas outside, so I wouldn't advise it. It sets an unhealthy precedent.

My infant is going to attend a wedding—should they dress up?

Yes. You don't need to dress them in a suit or black tie, of course, but festive attire should be worn—a romper with a collared shirt, perhaps, or a shirt and nice shorts.

My daughter is a flower girl. Do I get to suggest what she wears, or is it up to the bride?

It's the bride's special day and entirely her choice to dress them as she sees fit. It would be considered rude to make any suggestions, so if the outfit is not to your taste, just grin and bear it!

TRAVEL TIPS

"Whoever one is, and wherever one is, one is
always in the wrong if one is rude."

— MAURICE BARING

Even if you're a seasoned traveler, going anywhere with children is a challenge. You can imagine the experiences I've had after years of traveling with five of them! I recall a particular overnight flight when one of my sons was teething; he just cried and cried, and I couldn't get him to settle down. I walked around in circles in the galley, desperately trying to soothe him. Once the plane landed and after I had gone six hours with no sleep, a gentleman approached me and made a snide remark about how rude and inconsiderate I had been on the flight. This bothered me a great deal for quite a while. I had been very conscious of the comfort of my fellow passengers and had tried my best to keep my son away and in the galley. I wanted to tell this man that a baby is a baby—but I didn't. I'm sure most parents have been in similar situations, and no matter how prepared we think we are, we will all experience such incidents that are completely out of our control.

There are ways to avoid potential meltdowns when your child is older and an essential rule of travel etiquette is to make sure your child isn't bothering fellow passengers, as far as possible. When my children were little, I tried to achieve this by preparing a goody bag for each of them, to get them through the flight and keep them excited and engaged. When I parented my eldest, there weren't iPhones and other devices to distract them and we were able to make it through a flight. The goody bag, which can be filled with a notebook, sketch pad, and other old-school forms of entertainment, is a great way to alleviate dependency on the phone or device. Luckily, on most flights today, children can watch movies and television shows or play games on the airplane's in-flight entertainment system. Yet with all of these choices, there are still many challenges when traveling with a small child. Children are used to routines, and taking them off their schedule is never an easy task. It's truly worth the effort, though, because traveling introduces children to a new way of looking at the world.

I consider myself fortunate to have grown up abroad, in Hong Kong. It shaped my sense of the world, so I wanted to provide my children with similar global experiences. When I was young, my family traveled quite a distance to visit our grandparents who lived in America. This trip wasn't easy—my parents were traveling with three young children—but those memories of spending time with my family, as well as the memories of visiting new countries and cultures, are some of the best I have.

Don't worry—you don't have to jet-set around the globe to benefit from this mindset; you simply need to respect and embrace other cultures. Some have their own rules on etiquette, but before I get into those, let me share my house rules for traveling.

House Rules

Many of these rules are as applicable to traveling around the neighborhood as they are to short trips and longer outings.

Be considerate

It doesn't take much to be considerate. All you need to do is be thoughtful. When my children were younger, whenever we traveled or even when we were out and about in the city, I always reminded them to let others exit first before entering themselves—whether from elevators, trains, buses, restaurants, office buildings … pretty much anywhere. When exiting a plane, they knew they must wait their turn to leave their seats—no pushing or scrambling to get out first (there's nothing worse than someone pushing past you while you try to gather items from the overhead bin after a long flight). Another big no-no on a plane is letting your child kick the seat in front of them (we've all been on the receiving end of this, sadly) or fight loudly with a sibling. I insisted that my children keep their voices down on flights, as I never, ever wanted to be the mother with the child who is shouting and being rude.

In this age of noise-canceling headphones we need to be aware of how loud children can be, and make sure they use their indoor voices. Even though they might feel the plane is a relaxed setting, they should remember they are in a public space and be mindful of others.

Walk respectfully

Walking etiquette varies from culture to culture, so when you travel abroad, observe how others are walking up and down stairs and follow their lead. This avoids the potential for accidentally bumping into another person.

I made sure to let my kids know from a young age that they should stay to the right when walking up and down stairs in America, but that in England, it's the other way around. A friend's grown child reminded me of what a school in London would tell their students in order to remember this simple rule. They are taught the acronym CALM, which stands for *Courtesy Applies, Left Movement*—meaning always pass on the left.

A good way to reinforce this in the UK when walking up or down stairs that have banisters running along both sides is to always hold the handrail with your left hand. When you're on an escalator and standing still, you stay to the right: stand right, walk left. If someone wants to walk up at a faster pace and pass others, they must do it on the left (remember: left movement). See the illustration on the page opposite.

While walking on the street in America, pedestrians are expected to be polite. The rule again is to stay to the right; I doubt most people know this, but if everyone followed this practice, there would be no need to navigate a path through a crowded sidewalk, which, with children, can often be a hassle.

Road sense

If you're in a foreign country and are unsure of the proper side of the street to walk on, as a rule you can generally follow the same protocol used by drivers (drive on the left, walk on the left, for example).

Learn a few language essentials

Before you travel to another country, it's a good idea to teach your child how to say "Please," "Thank you," "Excuse me," and a few other useful words and phrases in the local language. It's really rather sweet to hear a child trying to incorporate a new language into their vocabulary, and it also shows that they are receptive to a new culture. You don't want to overwhelm them, though, so just focus on a handful of words, and they will hopefully be able to master them. Kids will be heartened to see how excited people are when they hear a child trying to speak in their language, especially if the child is being polite.

Be positive

Every trip will involve some sort of obstacle, and not every trip is a "vacation." If you are having a hard time dealing with relatives or if a hotel isn't quite what you envisaged when you booked it, try to focus on something positive. Remember: children need you, as a parent, to be positive, as they will feed off your energy. This sounds like simple advice, but remaining optimistic in less-than-ideal circumstances is a sign of good manners.

Communication is key when you are unhappy with a situation; let your child know that it's not impolite to complain or express their unhappiness, but they just have to do it in a thoughtful way. This also applies to parents who might lose their cool and scream at the waitstaff or a hotel clerk while their small child looks on. Your child is learning how to interact with others through your interactions with adults, so you must ensure you are able to express your emotions respectfully.

Even the best vacations can be hard for a child who misses their bed and some of their familiar comforts. Bringing a favorite toy from home can give your child a sense of security and help make the transition to the new location a happy one, because happiness keeps a little piece of comfort close.

THE BASICS

Every public interaction you partake in is an opportunity to set an example for how a family should behave. You don't want to be the loudest parent in a restaurant, for instance, or accidentally do something that might offend anyone. Children today don't need to be as polished and polite as, say, those of our parents' generation, and we certainly don't subscribe to the old adage "Children should be seen and not heard"; when children openly voice their opinions, their little personalities are allowed to shine through. This isn't the case in many parts of the world, however, so when you're visiting a foreign country, try to learn about their rules and customs before you travel, so that you can be sure to observe them when you are there.

Over the years, I have established a number of general rules worth noting when traveling abroad, which I will run through with you here.

Mind your manners

When staying at a hotel, be mindful of the people around you—and also below you. Tell your kids to try not to make too much noise, especially if you're like me and have a large family. (In the past I was reprimanded once or twice by hotel security for letting the boys run up and down their bedrooms bouncing a ball.) Also bear in mind that a hotel is like an apartment building and, although many hotels are child-friendly, that doesn't give kids carte blanche to misbehave. Children love to run into their new spaces and jump on beds, open closets—and don't forget the minibar and snacks! Make sure you set ground rules as to what is or isn't allowed.

Don't stare or point

When a child is taken out of their normal, everyday routine and
surroundings, they might be excited about the new people they are seeing
and forget their manners. This is why it's so important to teach them to
respect other cultures. If a child notices someone dressed in a different
style, for example, they need to be aware that it's impolite to point and
stare. Remind them that staring at someone for a long period—under any
circumstance—is considered bad manners. A way to help your child to
understand this is to ask them how they would feel if someone was
staring and pointing at them.

Be patient

Don't you find it funny how every impatient child seems absolutely fine in a movie theater or waiting in a long line for a ride at an amusement park, yet finds it impossible to sit still in a car or plane without being entertained? If you're going on a long journey, keep your child occupied with some of the suggestions I made earlier. (Remember my goody bag?) Pack a snack and some fun activities. It's also a good opportunity to get your kids to listen to audiobooks and to create a playlist together before you set off. Encourage your child to keep a sketch diary. Again, the key is to make these trips fun.

Making memories

My family still has a few playlists (called Road Trip 1, 2, and 3) from a few summers back that we used when traveling around the West Coast in an RV. They remind us fondly of that trip whenever we listen to them. Don't forget, your trips create memories that your children will hopefully treasure for years to come, so you want to make sure that they enjoy themselves. If the trip is stressful, then that's what the child will remember.

Be a polite houseguest

If you or your child are staying with another family while on your travels, it's polite to bring them a gift as a token of appreciation. Do your best to follow the rules of the house and be gracious to your host. At the risk of sounding like a broken record, remind your child to always say "Please" and "Thank you." Also be sure to keep your room tidy! You don't want your child to make a mess of someone else's house. A sign of excellent manners is a family (this includes the children) that offers to help clean up.

Dress appropriately

It's okay to dress comfortably for travel; I
would often put my children in sweatpants for
overnight flights, but I made sure they always
looked presentable and not sloppy. T-shirts are
fine, as are shorts when traveling on short
flights, but avoid letting your child wear
them on overnight flights, in case they
get cold. (Remember: your child will—
hopefully!—be going to sleep at some
point and planes can often get rather chilly.)

When traveling in other countries and visiting
local sights, be respectful. This is especially true
when visiting churches, temples, shrines, or
other places of worship. So that means no
short cut-off shorts, tank tops, or flip-flops.
In some countries, such as Greece and Italy,
shoulders should be covered when visiting a church; in other countries,
girls may be required to wear a headscarf. It's a good idea to check any rules
and regulations ahead of time, so that you can make sure you are wearing
appropriate clothing before you set off.

Etiquette around the globe

It helps to be aware of local customs and etiquette before you travel so that you don't get caught out or—worse still—end up accidentally causing offense! Here are a few examples, to give you an idea of the varying dos and don'ts around the world.

Be clean Wherever you go in the world, never, ever litter.

Eating late In some Mediterranean and western European countries, like Greece and Spain, dinner can sometimes start as late as 9:00 or 10:00 p.m., and it's often impossible to find restaurants open earlier than 8:00 p.m. Unlike in America, in these countries, children are welcome to dine at these nighttime meals, which are considered family affairs. While children who are used to eating earlier may find this change in routine a little hard to adjust to, most will usually look at it as an exciting treat to be allowed to stay up so late for dinner!

Watch your hands In Greece, it's considered rude to show the palm of your hand with your fingers spread out. (It actually means something quite offensive.)

Don't point In Asia, never, ever point your chopsticks at anyone.

Avoid signs of bad luck In Japan, don't leave your chopsticks sticking upright in the rice: this is considered bad luck.

NO   YES

Eat with your hands In parts of India and Malaysia, it's considered normal for people to eat with their hands, which can be quite fun—especially for kids.

Peel a weisswurst In Germany, the traditional way to eat a weisswurst is to peel it first and then cut it and eat it.

Use your utensils In Chile, you eat everything with a knife and fork—even food that you would consider to be finger food.

Cover your hair Most swimming pools in China require you to wear a bathing cap.

Shoes off! In Japan, it's polite to remove your shoes immediately upon entering a home.

Top Tips

My child has been invited to travel with another family. Do I offer the family money? How should I thank them?

Depending on the child's age, you might give the parent spending money for your child. If the child is older, they can be in control of their own spending money. You shouldn't offer to pay for the child, except for travel expenses. When your child returns, give the parents a thoughtful card together with a present; be creative when choosing the gift, as it's the thought that counts.

Is it considered bad manners to take a baby or toddler on an overnight flight?

Taking an overnight flight with a young child may be unavoidable, especially when flying a long haul. I actually prefer flying overnight with my kids from America to Europe because the flight is long enough for them to be able to sleep on the plane. Many children don't adjust well to jet lag, however, and suffer from nausea when they land. The key is knowing how your child reacts and planning accordingly. Be prepared to help them through their jet lag. Keep them well hydrated; sunshine and fresh air on arrival can also help.

Is it okay to change a diaper at your seat on a plane or bus?

It is impolite to change a diaper in a shared seat. However, if it's an emergency, try to find a private spot where you can place a changing pad down and change the child, and be discreet.

Should a child have any input on vacation planning?

Yes, but keep it limited. As touched on previously, your child will feel included if you present them with two or three options and let them choose one. I always let my kids pick something they'd like to do on a vacation, so they feel empowered and have something to look forward to. Also, children love routine, so it's nice to create a ritual of a recurring vacation.

Can a child wear a swimsuit to a meal at a vacation resort?

No, unless you are ordering a casual meal or snack at the pool from your beach chair, though even then, they should cover up, as it teaches them this rule from an early age. Children should always change into clean, dry clothes for a meal in a restaurant.

PLAYDATES

"Being considerate of others will take your
children further in life than any college degree."

— MARIAN WRIGHT EDELMAN

Playdates are an essential part of the development of children's social skills. While on a playdate, a child can learn either how to host or how to be a guest. When your child is a baby and throughout the toddler years, the parent is in charge of scheduling these get-togethers and choosing friends. But as your child gets older, they will make their own friends at school, and you will be sending them to friends' houses or to the homes of people whom you may only know through school functions. This is when a child begins their journey to independence, so giving them a healthy social foundation early on is vital to help them understand how to be a good friend.

When your child goes on a playdate, always find out who will be watching the children. Obviously a parent or caregiver will be there when they are very small, but as they get older, things become a little trickier. There have been countless articles demonizing the helicopter parent, and while you don't have to track your child's every move, you should be aware of who will be at the home they are visiting. One question worth asking is whether the hosting child has any elder siblings. I say this from experience as, a few years ago, an email was sent around my youngest son's class about an inappropriate video game being played on a playdate; the game was suitable for ages thirteen and over, and the children who played it were only six years old at the time. Many parents replied to the email in horror, myself included, agreeing that such games should have been put away, out of reach of the younger children. Further emails flew back and forth, and I quickly realized that the house they were talking about was mine and that my young son was the culprit!

I was mortified and immediately sent out my apologies. When you have a big family with children of different ages, you tend to host numerous playdates, and there will inevitably be some overlap. But the incident taught me an important lesson, and my older boys' video games are now stored safely away from my youngest. This is why I like to be aware of what my children will be up to at playdates.

With this in mind, when you're hosting a playdate you might want to contact the parent in advance, to ask them if watching a certain movie or playing a video game is okay with them. Some parents can also be picky about the food their children eat, and that's fine; ask them what they feel comfortable with, and this usually avoids any problems further down the line. After hosting two decades' worth of playdates—and still hosting them as I write this!—I have established some house rules for scheduling, hosting, and sending my children on them.

House Rules

Communicate with parents

When your child is old enough to be dropped off for a playdate, set a timeline—when to drop off and pick up. If hosting, limit how many children get together; I favor a total of two or four, as three can leave an odd one out.

When your child is hosting a playdate for the first time, make sure you explain that other children will be in their house and that those other children will be playing with their toys. (If there are toys that are special to your child, it's okay to put those away before a playdate arrives.) This can be difficult for young children to accept, but it is the ideal experience for teaching them how to share. The more you prepare your child, the more fun it will be for them. If you feel your child may struggle, consider doing some role-play to teach them how to act when they host a friend.

My children have been taught to ask me if it's okay before they accept a playdate or have one in the house. Once they mention the playdate, I always check with the other parent to set up a time for the pickup. If I'm running behind for any reason, I will always text the parent, and I expect the same courtesy when I am the host. Communication costs nothing, and staying in touch avoids any potential anxiety on the part of the child, parent, or both.

Older children often prefer to go to a house where there is less parental guidance, which means they won't be monitored when they play video games or surf the web. Make sure you are aware of who is at home in the hours after school. Although the parents might be responsible people, it's hard to keep an eye on an older child who is allowed to be home unsupervised or is watched by a teenage sibling or a nanny until the parents return home from work later in the day.

Ask permission

I have noticed that some of our children's friends—especially those who are regular visitors to our home—seem comfortable opening our kitchen cabinets and helping themselves to food. They will also turn on the TV and the like. While I love that they feel so comfortable in my home, I do expect, and find it polite, for children to ask permission before they open drawers or use anything in the house.

I once came home to find one of my children's friends happily tucking into a bowl of my favorite homemade Greek meatballs, which I had been looking forward to eating all day. If you're a parent of older kids, you have

no doubt had similar experiences. This led me to have a family discussion on friends, playdates, and boundaries. Friends of my children can help themselves to the designated playdate snack tray in the kitchen or pantry, but they should really ask before they help themselves to anything in the refrigerator. Placing food that is okay to share in a designated section of your pantry helps avoid any awkward discussions on what your child is allowed to offer their friends.

Healthy snacks

My family tries to follow healthy eating habits, and I limit my children's exposure to unhealthy and sugary foods. When I host a playdate, I offer only healthy treats; I don't want to give the children too much sugar, as it can make them unruly and overly energetic! I also tell my children that if another parent is more lenient with sugar-filled treats, they should take only one.

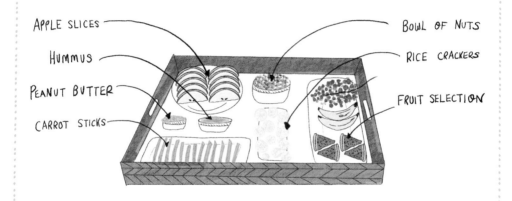

APPLE SLICES

HUMMUS

PEANUT BUTTER

CARROT STICKS

BOWL OF NUTS

RICE CRACKERS

FRUIT SELECTION

If your child has a food allergy or dietary restriction, it's vital that you alert the person hosting the playdate. I have firsthand experience of this, and I always make sure my son has his EpiPen with him. I remind the parent who is hosting and let my son know that he must also remind the parent himself that he is allergic to certain foods.

Clean up

We've all walked into a child's room an hour into a playdate only to see that every single toy has been removed from the shelf and scattered across the floor. If the children make a mess, they should be taught to put the toys away. I want my children to clean up whatever mess they make at home (doubly so at someone else's house!), and I want them to work with their friends to tidy up. If the children are babies or toddlers, the parent accompanying the child should offer to help clean up the toys.

THE BASICS

Now that we've looked at the rules at my house,
here are some general guidelines for having
successful—and civil—playdates.

Arranging a date

Playdates can be arranged by email, by text, or in person. If your child asks at school pickup to have a playdate with another child, it is not impolite to refuse such an impromptu invitation. Let the child and their parent or caregiver know that it isn't an ideal time—that your child has a sports game or other engagement—and arrange a date for another day.

Additionally, when arranging playdates for younger children, it's important to discuss whether the other parent is to stay for the date. Elementary-school-aged children can be dropped off and picked up, but many preschool children want their parents to stay with them. Some children get teary when their parent leaves, so be sure you've prepared for this and have the parent's information at hand, so you can reach out if they need to come and pick up their child.

Hosting the parent

Unless you invited the parent to stay for lunch beforehand, you don't have to lay out a full-blown meal, but do be courteous and offer them a drink and a snack. Talk to them and be a gracious host. On most playdates, parents' conversations usually revolve around parenting and school. If you do have work to do or need to start preparing dinner, let the parent know, and politely excuse yourself. Before you leave, make sure that they're comfortable and don't feel offended.

Playdates shouldn't last for hours, and you should never overstay your welcome. Two hours on a weekday is fine, as the kids will have homework, but you can make the playdates longer on weekends.

Greetings

I've noticed that many of the children who come to my house seem confused about how they should address me. I tell my children's friends to call me MC; I know other parents prefer to be called Mr. or Mrs. when addressed. As mentioned in Chapter 2, the best thing to do is simply ask. If your child doesn't know how to address their friend's parent, teach them to say, "Excuse me, what should I call you?" When in doubt, however, it's always safest to call parents by their last name unless otherwise instructed.

Children should also be respectful toward their friends' parents and try to not say inappropriate things in front of them. Make sure they know to look a person in the eye when they greet them and to shake an adult's hand when saying hello or leaving.

Behavior

It goes without saying that children should be on their best behavior while on a playdate! If a child starts acting out or you notice them bullying or being unkind to your child, it is absolutely appropriate to intervene. You don't have the right to discipline another child, but you may tell them that their actions are upsetting, and ask their parent to pick them up early. Alert the parent to the bullying. This is a serious issue, and parents need to take responsibility for their child's actions.

Remember that playdates provide an ideal opportunity for children to learn to share and to understand that they need to consider others' feelings. That is how their social skills develop. By calmly explaining what is and isn't acceptable behavior, should any disagreements arise, you are helping to lay the foundations for them to grow into compassionate and thoughtful human beings.

Saying goodbye

We've all experienced the child who pleads to stay "just a little bit longer" when it comes time to leave. Some kids will do anything to prolong the visit—even insult their parents and call them mean for picking them up too early! Children need to learn that all good things must come to an end and that they should be courteous and not kick up a fuss when it's time to go. You don't want them making a big drama out of it. Remind them to be considerate by helping to clean up any mess before they go and by thanking the adult for hosting them.

Reciprocating

If a child is repeatedly going to a friend's house, it's important to reciprocate and host a playdate at your home. Never take advantage of a fellow parent! If a child isn't comfortable going on playdates at another person's home, don't be offended. Let the parent know you are always happy to host when their child feels ready to be on their own.

Sleepovers

When your child is older, you'll start hosting sleepovers—which brings with it a whole new range of issues. If a child gets homesick and you can't calm them down, contact the parent no matter what time it is, as it can be quite traumatizing for a child, especially on those first sleepovers. I can't tell you how many times my husband had to get out of bed to pick up a homesick child in the middle of the night. Also contact the parents immediately if the child is sick or injured in any way.

Top Tips

What do I do if my child is upset that they weren't invited to a playdate?

It's always painful to see a child upset, and the best way to approach this is to explain that they can't be invited on every playdate. Don't call the parent or make a big fuss. If the child wants to foster a relationship with the other child, try hosting a playdate at your house instead.

My child's friend breaks a toy every time they come over. Is it in bad taste to ask for a replacement from the parent?

Children can be clumsy and will inevitably break things at times. If it's done intentionally and with malice, you should approach the parent. If not, unless it's a collectible or something of value, just mention it to the parent but don't ask for a replacement. In any case, the child who is responsible should learn to apologize for causing damage. It's not impolite to break things by mistake, but it is impolite not to say sorry.

Is there a specific age when I can drop my child off at a playdate? If I am anxious and want to stay, is that okay?

Raise this issue with the hosting parent by telling them that you're feeling anxious. You might want to stay for a short while and leave when your child is comfortable. Let the parent know that you are reachable. If your child is under three, you might want to stay close.

I want to raise my child as a healthy eater and limit their sugar intake. Is it rude to ask the host of the playdate to avoid offering unhealthy snacks?

It's okay to ask within reason, but not very polite if it makes the playdate uncomfortable for everyone else—unless the child has a medical issue, in which case be sure to mention any dietary restrictions.

Is it rude to say no if someone is dropping off a sick child?

You have the right to refuse a sick child. It's also good form for a parent to mention if the child has a sibling at home with strep throat, stomach flu, and so on, as no one wants to be responsible for making another child sick.

PARTY ESSENTIALS

"Saying thank you is more than good manners.
It is good spirituality."

— ALFRED PAINTER

My mother always went out of her way to be creative for our birthday parties. She loved themed parties and hosted many for our family members. One year she threw a fabulous outdoor picnic party for me, complete with little wicker baskets and red gingham napkins and tablecloths. Another year, she was ahead of her time and threw a Disney-themed party, at which every child was given a classic Mickey Mouse mask. Putting this party together was no mean feat given that I grew up in Hong Kong in the seventies and Disney was yet to become the global empire it is today. Looking back, I've inherited my mother's passion for hosting. I'll confess we both obsess over details, but more importantly, we simply want everyone to have a wonderful time. I learned from my mother what it means to be generous of heart and that throwing a party isn't about overindulging your child, but rather a thoughtful gesture toward others.

Sometimes kids can become overly focused on the presents or parents can get preoccupied planning the perfect party, but we mustn't lose sight of the reason we throw parties in the first place: to have a good time and celebrate with the people we care about. On a positive note, I've noticed a growing tendency for parents to scale back on these over-the-top parties. In fact, many of my young son's friends' parents ask that children not bring presents.

This trend reminds me of spending the last few days of summer at my grandmother's house outside of Boston when I was a child. My birthday is in September, so my grandmother would always throw a birthday party for me and invite some of the children in her neighborhood. At the end of the party, she would tell me that I could choose one present to keep. The presents were still wrapped and I wasn't allowed to know who had given them. Once I'd picked one, she would distribute the remainder of the presents to the birthday guests. When I was younger, it was hard for me to understand why she did this. Just as any child would, I questioned her. She explained that I was fortunate enough to have all the toys I needed, and that I should think of others and always be generous. This idea of giving back, and of thinking how I can make other people happy, was one of the biggest gifts my grandmother ever gave me.

There is much etiquette surrounding parties and the different rules for maintaining proper manners, such as when to send a thank-you card or note and how to respond to an invitation. We will discuss these, of course, but to me, one of the most important aspects is to make the party a memorable affair for everyone. This means making sure that your child is well-mannered and good-natured, and that—if they are the host—they ensure everyone feels welcome at the celebration.

House Rules

As a mother of five, I have been involved in more children's birthday parties than the average parent, so here are some of my favorite house rules for a thoughtful party plan, based on many years of experience as both a host and the mother of a guest.

Be a kind host

Even though 99 percent of party planning falls upon the parents, remember it's still your child's party. You can give out the best goody bags, but if your child is rude or misbehaves, the party won't be a success. I would often remind my children to be courteous, to thank their friends for coming, and to make sure no one is ever left out. Once they feel that everyone is having a good time, they can then enjoy themselves.

Older children might have friends from different schools or camps, or from their sports teams, and it can be hard for them to balance having a variety of friends at their party. To help them out, I always stay around to ensure that every detail is in place, but also to supervise and check that everyone is happy. If one of the guests doesn't seem to be having a good time, encourage your child to include them in an activity or game.

Invitations

Unfortunately, people hardly send paper invitations anymore. I used to love receiving and scrapbooking them, but now we get most invitations through email and text. It's not rude to send an invitation to a party or formal event in these digital formats. I would recommend taking the time to make the invitation special. Personally, texts seem abrupt, and you might want to embellish it instead of sending a flat text. For instance, you can sign up for various platforms that help you design text or email invitations.

Répondez s'il vous Plaît
(WHICH MEANS PLEASE REPLY)

Reply on time

Parents are responsible for accepting or declining an invitation to a child's party. Be sure to try to RSVP as soon as possible; if you are the host and someone doesn't respond, it's okay to call or send a text and check in. If your child gets invited to another party at the same time (you'd be surprised how often this happens!), the proper rule is to attend the one you accepted first. A good solution to a double invite is to plan another activity or a playdate to celebrate the other child's birthday. It's also customary to apologize and explain that your child couldn't attend because of another commitment.

If you RSVP "yes," you have to show up. At one of my childhood parties, two girls who had said that they were coming never appeared. I was so disappointed. They didn't apologize, and even though it's been decades since that party, I still recall the feeling of being hurt. If your child has sent an RSVP stating that they will attend but, for some reason, cannot make it, let the parent know. Similarly, if your child had been unable to go to a party due to a trip or prior engagement that has suddenly been canceled, it's okay to reach out to the parent and ask if your child could still attend, despite their initial RSVP.

I have been guilty of losing email invites in my inbox when I haven't responded immediately, so when you get an invitation, reply promptly, and then it won't get buried in a plethora of messages. If you do miss one (it happens), simply apologize. Remember that someone is going out of their way to organize and host a party, and no matter how close—or otherwise—your child is to the person who has invited them, it is always good manners to respond.

YES

"THANK YOU SO MUCH FOR HAVING ME."

Be a thoughtful guest

You don't want to be the parent who picks up their child from a party and finds out they had a tantrum or bullied someone. It's important to teach children to treat others—and others' homes—with respect. I know I've said it before, but I told my children to always say "Please" and "Thank you," to never forget to say goodbye before they leave, and to always shake hands and thank the host and tell them how much they enjoyed the party. If you do have a child who is extremely competitive or a bit of an extrovert, remind them that a party is about everyone having fun, not just them.

Write a thank-you note

Even though my children are older, I'm still getting thank-you notes from their friends, which I love. And it warms my heart to hear other adults tell me they received thank-you cards from my children. When my children were growing up, I expected them to say their thank-yous upon leaving a party but—importantly—to also write thank-you cards after they received presents. Getting your child to sit down and write one isn't an easy task, but it is such a lovely gesture toward a guest who has gone out of their way. A handwritten thank-you is a way of teaching your child about being thankful and showing gratitude and, in a world of technology, is something to be cherished.

If you are throwing a standard birthday party, your child could send a thank-you note via an email or card. If your child is too young to write, you can be a bit more inventive: a friend had her child make a short video thanking the guests for attending the party and for the presents they brought. Or you could have your child draw a picture as a thank-you. No matter what you choose to do as a family, a gift should be acknowledged with some form of thanks.

The conventional length of time for sending out a thank-you note is no more than two weeks. However, when it comes to a thank-you letter, it's always better late than never. You might want to purchase stationery to encourage children to write a handwritten thank-you card. This discipline not only serves them well in the future, but is also a good exercise for practicing their handwriting and signature.

How to say thank you

FORMAL PARTY

DEAR MR. & MRS...........
DEAR AUNTIE & UNCLE
THANK YOU FOR TAKING
PART IN THIS MEMORABLE DAY.
HAVING YOU THERE WAS.........

Love From

....

SLEEPOVER

DEAR...........
THANK YOU FOR THE
FUN SLEEPOVER.
YOUR HOUSE IS THE
BEST FOR SLEEPOVERS...

Love From

....

GIFT

DEAR................
THANK YOU FOR THE

....
(NAME THE GIFT)

Love From

....

CASH PRESENT

DEAR ....

THANK YOU FOR THE
GENEROUS GIFT...

Love From

....

BIRTHDAY PARTY

DEAR.................
THANK YOU FOR THE LOVELY
BIRTHDAY YOU THREW FOR.......
I HAD SUCH A FUN TIME.

Love From

....

Wondering how many children should be invited to a party or if presents should be opened during the festivities? Here are the basic rules for party etiquette.

Guest list

There are numerous rules floating around about how many people you should invite to your child's birthday party. Some parenting experts suggest as many guests as the child's age plus one. That works until the age of three or four, after which children usually want a larger party.

My advice would be to work with your child on creating a guest list—and be realistic.

It really all comes down to how many you can handle. Where will you throw the party? At home? If so, could you entertain a large group of rowdy kids in dress-up?

If you can't accommodate an entire class and want to have only a handful of kids over, it isn't considered rude not to invite everyone. Do teach your child to be considerate of others' feelings, though, and discourage them from bragging about a big party when not everyone is invited.

How many guests?

First birthday party This is an important birthday, but the party is for the parents not the baby. You can also limit the guest list to close friends and family, as you don't want to overwhelm your baby. Remember: this party is a special one, at which lots of pictures will be taken. I kept my children's first parties relatively small—just four or five one-year-olds in high chairs around a table.

Preschool party For your preschooler's birthday, you might have to invite the entire school class. If this is too overwhelming, consider throwing a party in class or having two separate parties—one for your child's school friends and another for family and other friends.

Sleepover party Limit this to six children maximum! It's not a case of the number of guests being a reflection of your child's popularity but rather a number you are able to control and handle. I found that it's always best to stick with an even number; four was my ideal. Make it fun and be creative—your child will treasure the memories.

Formal event Like all formal events, your guest list should consist of close friends and family. These can be large affairs, especially if it's a religious celebration, but don't feel pressure to invite everyone. It's not bad manners to invite just the number of people you can manage; after all, a party should be fun and not stressful. If you're anxious about it, your child will pick up on your energy. Remember: it's called a celebration because you are marking a special occasion. Parties are supposed to be enjoyable, so be mindful of this when planning them.

Giving and receiving gifts

Children should bring a gift for a party unless otherwise specified on the invite. It is acceptable for the child whose celebration it is to open gifts at the party, but I would suggest doing this only when the child is old enough to control their emotions. If they are disappointed with a gift, they shouldn't show it. Explain this to your child beforehand. A young child who has been taught not to lie might be confused by this idea, so let them know that in instances such as this, they need to be considerate of their friend's feelings and not offend them. If they really don't like the gift, you can talk about places to donate the present afterward. (I don't suggest recycling gifts by giving them to another child for their birthday, as you might forget who gave you the present and it could end up back in the hands of the original child.)

If two people give your child the same gift, you are responsible for returning the gift, not the person who gave it. Gift cards are acceptable presents and are often the preferred choice for tweens and teens.

I love wrapping presents and have always gone out of my way to be creative, but it isn't necessary to go over the top. As long as you demonstrate that you've given it some consideration, your efforts will be appreciated regardless of how elaborate the end result.

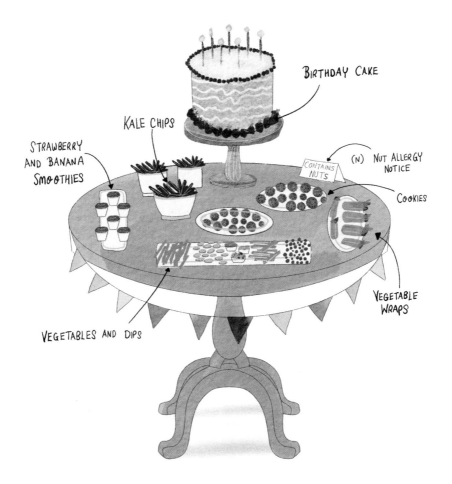

BIRTHDAY CAKE

KALE CHIPS

STRAWBERRY
AND BANANA
SMOOTHIES

CONTAINS
NUTS

(N) NUT ALLERGY
NOTICE

COOKIES

VEGETABLE
WRAPS

VEGETABLES AND DIPS

Serving food

Every party should have food for the children, even if it's just snacks; you want to be a good—and generous—host, after all. If you're hosting a party in between mealtimes, be sure to provide healthy nibbles in addition to the birthday cake. It's now considered the norm to ask guests if they have any food allergies. Similarly, if your child has an allergy, alert the host and send the child with appropriate foods for them to eat.

Time frame

On average, a child's party should last around two hours. Parents should indicate the drop-off and pickup times; be on time for both! Parties often include organized activities, and being late without alerting the host might throw off the party's schedule. Whenever I hosted parties on a weekend I would let the party run longer: it could be a lunch, say, with a pick-up around 4:00 p.m.

Formal parties

When you take your child to a formal party, like a wedding or a baby shower, they are going to come into contact with adults they haven't met before. Conventional etiquette for a proper introduction is for the child to shake hands with the adult and make eye contact, but wait for the adult to introduce themselves rather than asking them their name. It's also important to teach your child that, if seated, it's considered polite to stand when being introduced—and that this rule applies at any age. (See also Chapter 7, page 146.)

Some formal parties and dinners have you sign a guest book at the event. This is also an ideal time for a child to write their signature and show their appreciation for the host. Personally, I love this tradition, and when I was living in England, I found this to be a common practice at formal dinner parties or when visiting someone's home for the weekend. If you're hosting an event, you might consider having a guest book because it's a simple way to have a special memento from the event or to look back and see all the visitors you've had over the years.

At formal events, children are usually seated at their own table. If your child doesn't know any of the other children, you might want to spend some time at their table helping them to adjust to this new situation. Remind them to be mindful and respectful of the proceedings during any ceremonies, to whisper if they have to speak, and never to take out electronics during a wedding, christening, or religious service of any kind.

Top Tips

My child has been invited to a party. Can I bring their sibling?

If you have another child who wasn't invited, don't assume that they can stay. Parents plan for a certain number of guests and bringing an extra child may be viewed as bad manners, especially if you just expect to be able to leave them there. If you do bring along a sibling and the host insists they stay, make sure they're not just saying it to be polite. You don't want to be known as the parent who always drops off their kids at parties so they can run their errands.

My child wasn't invited to a friend's birthday party. Should I contact the parent?

In short, no. We've all been there. If your child doesn't get invited, don't get upset. This is an instructive experience for them. We can't get invited to every party or event. Remind your child that there were also children who were left off of their guest lists and that this happens to everybody.

My child was invited to a drop-off party but wants me to stay. Is this okay?

Tell the host that your child is having an issue and see how they feel about letting you stick around. Let them know that you'll leave once your child settles down, and make yourself helpful in the meantime. Most parents will be understanding and genuinely quite thankful for the extra set of hands.

Is there an average price one should spend on a birthday gift?

I am a firm believer in the adage that it's the thought that counts. If your child is close to the person in question, make it a meaningful gift that shows you have put a bit of effort into it. Don't forget that this is teaching your child to be generous of spirit too, so involve them in choosing a gift. Make it special; it can also be cute if it's something homemade.

The invitation specifies no gifts. Is it rude to bring a small present for the child?

If you are close to the family then it isn't rude, especially if it's something personal, but I wouldn't walk in bearing a massive box with a big bow on it, as it may embarrass other parents who came empty-handed as instructed. Another option would be to give the child a present at a separate time.

BEING A
GOOD SPORT

"Politeness and consideration for others is like
investing pennies and getting dollars back."

— THOMAS SOWELL

When my two eldest were young children, I was lucky enough to get some good advice from a friend of ours who was an athlete. He suggested choosing both a team sport and a martial art when picking sports for a young child. The reasoning behind this combination was that a team sport teaches a child to be a good team player, while the martial art fosters personal discipline. I followed his advice faithfully for all of my children: we chose a variety of team sports for them but enrolled all of them in judo. I loved the idea of how it would guide them toward "being a good sport." The concept of being a good sport is, of course, not solely related to athletic activities. It is a principle that should be applied in every aspect of life, which is why it's so important for children to learn it at an early age.

As I've mentioned before, being kind to yourself and others is the foundation of good manners. From hosting birthday parties where the guests feel as celebrated as the birthday boy or girl to always remembering to say thank you—these are just a few ways that your child can be a good sport off the field as well as on. It also means learning how to act respectfully in front of others. Children are known for throwing tantrums—but we all know adults (possibly including ourselves!) who still exhibit childlike outbursts from time to time, when placed in uncomfortable situations.

A few generations back, parents wouldn't allow children to show their emotions, and unfortunately this message is often instilled in boys even today. Although withholding emotion was once a sign of good manners, it is a concept I have never agreed with. I believe we shouldn't suppress our feelings. That said, it's also important to understand how our emotions might impact and affect others. This is where emotional intelligence comes into play.

After reading about the role emotional intelligence—a concept credited to renowned psychologist and science journalist Daniel Goleman, who popularized the term in 1995— plays in our lives, I did some research on the subject and wrote a post about it on my blog. Children who are taught how to process emotions properly tend to have a better sense of self and have an easier time working through their emotions and dealing with others. I compare the skills we learn in order to become emotionally intelligent to owning a toolbox that helps us problem-solve and cope with day-to-day issues. I call this a "happiness toolbox," and I have filled our family toolbox with essential tools to help build emotional well-being, such as empathy, gratitude, and compassion. I came up with my own interpretation of these tools when I devised my house rules, which I will share with you now.

House Rules

Being a good sport goes beyond remembering to say "good job" when a friend's team scores the winning goal and your team loses. It's a mindset that our children will hopefully carry with them well into adulthood.

> To teach my kids how to be good sports, I came
> up with this list of house rules.

Be empathetic

Sometimes children's emotions can be so intense that it seems almost comical to try to appease them by telling them to be empathetic. Yet I do this for many reasons. For one, it gets the child to understand how others might be feeling. When my children were younger and if one of them confessed how upset they were with their friends due to an argument or other issue, I would have asked them how their friend might have viewed that particular interaction. I always noted that when they paused to think about the event from another's perspective, they usually calmed down and realized that they weren't the only person experiencing that moment.

That said, I don't advise prohibiting your child from having negative emotions, and I recognized when one of my children was upset. Healthy emotional intelligence, however, will help them to process and regulate their emotions a lot more easily. Friends will inevitably still fall out or disagree with one another every now and then, but by learning to consider others' points of view, children begin to forge a vital tool in helping them to be good sports.

Pet power

A valuable way to learn how to nurture and care about another being is by owning a pet. As a serious pet lover—I have six dogs and a goldfish!—I believe that having a pet can help foster empathy. You don't have to rush out and get a Great Dane, but owning something even as small as our goldfish teaches a child about responsibility and caring for another living creature.

Petiquette

It can be hard to resist reaching out to pet a passing pooch when you're a dog lover, but it's bad form to stroke a stranger's dog without first seeking consent from the owner (and the dog). Not only is it impolite, but there are safety considerations to bear in mind too. The dog may look friendly, but you don't know its background; it may be nervous around children, for example, or feel threatened by strangers approaching.

Follow these three steps to ensure that everyone is comfortable with the situation:

1. Ask the owner's permission.

2. Approach slowly and let the dog sniff you. If the dog reacts positively, it's okay to proceed.

3. Keep it brief! You don't want to overwhelm the dog—plus the owner probably has somewhere else to be.

NO

"HOW ARE YOU?"

"GOOD."

YES

"HOW ARE YOU?"

"I'M VERY WELL, THANK YOU. HOW ARE YOU?"

Proper introductions
(with eye contact!)

We touched on this in Chapter 6 with regard to formal parties, but its importance cannot be stressed enough, as it is a cornerstone of good manners. When my children were little and I was introducing them to an adult for the first time, they were expected to to shake hands, look the person in the eye, and introduce themselves. This is easier said than done, and I still sometimes have to remind my children to stand up, shake hands, or kiss the adult on the cheek if the situation warrants it. But, more importantly, I wanted my children to make eye contact. This shows the other person that we are interested and engaged—which brings me to my next rule: be an engaged listener.

Be an engaged listener

Children should be taught not only to communicate well but also to be good listeners—an especially valuable skill to develop in their formative years. Leading by example is key. I've been in restaurants where mothers are busy staring at their phones while their toddlers are similarly transfixed by iPads. If you want your child to be an engaged listener, put away the screens and start a conversation. It's also important to teach them that if there is a difference of opinion during a conversation they should attempt to engage in polite discourse rather than arguing aggressively (something that many adults appear to struggle with, sadly!). Children can be very opinionated and love sharing their viewpoints with others, but they need to understand that their views might not always be well received.

Let me give you an example. When they were growing up, if my children disliked a particular sports team or TV show but their friend loved it, I taught them to do their best to accept their friend's way of thinking and not insult their friend's interests. While the old saying that politics and religion should never be discussed in polite company isn't exactly child-focused, the principle still applies, so I do try to go over appropriate and inappropriate conversation topics with them. I always remind them, even now that they are teens and young adults, that everyone is entitled to a polite opinion.

Don't be envious

We've all experienced envy at some point in our lives. For kids, it can be as simple as being envious that a friend's parent allows them to eat more sugary snacks, or resenting a friend for always being on the winning team. There will be many times in your child's life when they'll find themselves feeling this emotion. The key is to teach them to be happy for their friends—not an easy thing to explain to a child who is upset, of course.

Try to help your child build self-esteem; when a child feels secure, they are less likely to feel envious. Insecurity can also lead to your child being jealous of their friends for having other friends, which can be damaging to both themselves and their relationships.

Keep it clean

We looked at personal hygiene and the importance of being clean and presentable in Chapter 3, but children need to learn that cleanliness also applies to their personal space: their bedroom, their home, and their own immediate environment. It even applies to dining out; just because you're being served doesn't mean that you should leave the table in a mess. Remind your kids that littering is always bad manners—under any circumstances—and that garbage cans should be used appropriately. Cleanliness is a mindset, and getting your kids into the habit in their early years will set them on the right path for later life.

Bless you!

Teaching children to be mindful of others when coughing and sneezing isn't just polite—it's common sense (after all, what could be more impolite than spreading germs everywhere!). Most of us were taught to cough into our hands, but unless you're holding a tissue, you may still end up spreading germs—from your hand to a doorknob, handrail, or just about any other thing you might touch while out in public.

The accepted advice these days is, when caught without a tissue, to cough into your upper arm/elbow, as this avoids the issue of passing on germs via your hands. It might not look great if you're sneezing into your elbow when in the company of the King, but better that than giving him a cold! Whatever the situation, make sure your children know to wash their hands afterward if facilities are available, or offer them hand sanitizer.

THE BASICS

There are basic rules for being a good sport. They range from knowing how to communicate to learning to accept your losses. While this book is aimed at parents as a guide for teaching their children, these rules also serve as pertinent reminders for adults and are ones that I try to follow myself, to the best of my ability.

Adults can find it hard to be a good sport. We sometimes see it on sports fields or at games where a determined or overly focused parent gets into an argument with another parent. Field games are meant to be for our children's enjoyment and benefit, so don't lose sight of how our kids would expect us to behave. Their coach wouldn't act like that, so why should you? I know of a soccer league that makes parents sign a pledge that they will behave while watching the kids play. Remember: you are their coach in life, so conduct yourself properly and be a role model.

No screaming or cursing

There is nothing more unattractive than a child who uses obscenities! A child shouldn't swear. This is a bad habit and is partly due to the fact that many adults swear near or around their children. Be mindful of what you say when your children are within earshot. If they hear you cursing, they will find it normal and mimic your behavior. Also, children have more access to streaming services and social media, which means they might be exposed to sophisticated language that they don't understand.

Don't gossip or tell lies

There is an entire industry built around gossip magazines and websites, so it's hard to tell a child that nobody gossips. You can, however, explain that it's a bad habit and may not only harm their relationships with their friends (most gossips eventually get caught out) but can also cause irreparable damage to someone's reputation. If they understand that gossiping could lead to their potentially losing a friend's trust—something that is then very difficult to rebuild—they might think twice about doing it in the first place.

Lying is another common issue that parents have to deal with. We've all caught our kids in a lie, whether it's the tell-tale crumbs on the kitchen counter accompanied by a child's vehement denial that they've eaten a cookie or the affirmative response you get when you ask if they've done their homework when you know full well that they haven't yet set foot in their room since getting home from school. Parenting experts recommend addressing each instance when you catch your child lying, in order to teach them that it's not an acceptable way to communicate and can be harmful. Don't shame them; simply explain that it's always better to tell the truth, even about something as seemingly inconsequential as taking a cookie without permission.

Rather complicatedly, of course, there are exceptions in the form of telling a white lie so as not to hurt someone else's feelings. We discussed this in Chapter 6, in relation to birthday gifts, but the same principle also applies to everyday situations. Try to make your child aware of the distinction.

Accept your losses

Losing is never easy at any age, but when you're young it can be especially hard to come in last or, say, lose three games in a row at chess or cards. In a large family, the younger children may often feel as though they'll never win a game. Just remind them that being able to accept a loss builds resilience—plus, practice makes perfect, which means they will need to accept a certain number of setbacks in order to advance in their sport or hobby. Never set the bar too high for your child, though; if you do, and they crash, then they might feel they have disappointed you. Let them lead the way while gently motivating them.

If a child feels they aren't doing well at a sport or a musical instrument, let them know they can actually learn more from rejection or failure than from success. However, you might want to find something they excel at, like another sport or even chess, to help them feel confident.

Lead by example—and no cheating!

Unsurprisingly, a good way to teach your child about winning
and losing is through playing a game. In my family, we often have
volleyball matches in which all the cousins, fathers, and uncles
participate. It's important for children to see that their parents—
and other adults—can lose games and be good losers. That way,
the adults are able to lead by example. Similarly, show your
children that there is never a reason to cheat, and that any victory
achieved through cheating is unfair not only to the
other people involved, but also to themselves.

Never brag

Being a braggart or continually boasting is considered ill-mannered and will
make your child quite unpopular, fast. Just because they've won the award
for the best math student in school or own the largest collection of designer
sneakers in their class, that doesn't mean they should gloat about it. Bear in
mind that a child might not be aware that they are gloating and upsetting
others, so it's important to point out this behavior. Bragging is often rooted
in insecurity, so there may be underlying issues relating to lack of self-
confidence and low self-esteem. Try to help your child to feel more secure
in what appear to be their vulnerable areas; as I always tell my children,
people don't need to list their accomplishments or boast about grades to
make friends.

Be a problem solver, not a problem maker

Teach your child that if they encounter a problem, the best way forward is to learn to find a way to solve it with the help of their friends, rather than just ignoring it or even actively making the situation worse. Say they're at a party and have been asked to participate in an art project that a few of the children aren't thrilled with. Even if they're not exactly over the moon about it themselves, instead of just agreeing with the children who are complaining (i.e., joining the problem makers) they should find the positives in the situation and offer a possible solution—in this instance, perhaps explaining to the other children that they should just try to make the best of it, or, alternatively, suggesting to the host a slightly different approach that might be more popular with the guests at the party.

Teaching a child the importance of self-advocacy—standing up both for themselves and for their friends—and to always look for a solution if something doesn't feel quite right will prepare them for dealing with the inevitable problems and issues that arise in adult life.

Addressing extreme behavior

If your child is aggressive and possibly bullying other children, try to find out what triggers this type of behavior and deal with it immediately, before it becomes a problem. Some preschool children have issues with biting; if this is the case with your child, keep a close eye on them when they're in a playground or on a playdate. If your child bites, hits, or throws things at another child, it's important you teach them to apologize. Children tend to bite when they're frustrated or when they can't process big emotions, though this can be difficult to explain to very young children, as they might not understand what they have done wrong. If your child has attacked another, be sure to express your concern and exchange information with the parent of the other child.

Time-out tactics

A good old-fashioned "time-out" can be a valuable tool for dealing with unruly behavior. I used a time-out chair when my first three children were aged four, six, and eight respectively. The four-year-old, especially, was quite cheeky, so when a time-out was needed, I would put him on the chair and make him sit quietly and reflect on what he did. (As a rule, I would make them sit for the number of minutes equivalent to their age.) This would usually clear up a tantrum or the need for a further time-out. Sometimes, however, I would go to get him when the time was up, and he would tell me that he wasn't finished with his time-out and that he needed a few more minutes! Either he was trying to regain control of the situation or he was incredibly self-aware—probably a bit of both—but in any case, the old-fashioned time-out always worked.

If you're unable to have a physical time-out in public, you might want to try a verbal one instead. For example, my girlfriends and I have a code word that we use when we dine together if one of us has salad or other greens stuck in our teeth. While obviously not employed as a behavioral time-out in our case, the same code-word principle can apply: if your child is misbehaving in public, you could use a mutually agreed-upon word to let them know that it isn't acceptable behavior and that you will not engage with them until they have calmed down.

Dealing with difference

The world is more connected today than ever before, one of the benefits being that children are now generally more accepting of others. Kids are exposed to a wide range of people and family situations on television, online, and in real life. In addition, schools are becoming more disability/difference aware, often facilitating discussion groups on differences and emotions. Our children will hopefully grow up to live in a society where people are accepted for who they are, rather than judged by what they believe, their lifestyle choices, their gender preferences, or whether they have the same abilities as others.

That said, when children encounter people who are different from them in some way, they might inadvertently react in a manner that could be perceived as rude or upsetting. It's therefore important to have conversations with your child to teach them that everyone is equal and that many children (and adults) face challenges that your child hasn't experienced. When you open a discussion, let your child ask questions—and listen to their concerns. Remember: they will be looking to you for guidance, so now is the time to set the benchmark for compassion and understanding in all dealings with others. The bottom line is that no one should ever be treated unkindly or with indifference.

TOP TIPS

My child is on a soccer team that never wins. He wants to quit the team—should I let him?

If you give in too easily when your child hasn't devoted enough time and effort to a sport, musical instrument, or activity, then you aren't teaching your child a good lesson. When the going gets tough later on in life, they won't be able to just walk away from something they don't like, will they?

My daughter's friend was bullying her. Can I address this girl about her behavior, or should I talk to the parents?

It's best to approach the parent, as a child shouldn't really have another parent talking to them about an issue. It may be seen as parent bullying—when an adult puts a child in a situation in which they're not mature enough to defend themselves—so keep any discussion between adults.

How do I tell my ten-year-old not to announce to everyone that they've taken a fancy trip or gotten the latest electronic device? I'd like to teach them not to brag.

Nobody likes a braggart. Tell your child to keep conversations about their lifestyle to a minimum. It's hard to balance what you share and what you don't, especially today with social media. Try to be an example to your child by showing them how you behave when discussing similar events.

I have a friend who curses in front of our kids. I don't like this behavior—how do I broach the subject with her?

If this bothers you—and it should—talk to your friend about it. Nobody wants to hear a little child cursing, and that's what will happen if your child continually overhears bad language. Tell your friend that it's having a negative effect on your child and to be mindful around them.

We have a dog and had a situation where a guest was mean to the dog. My child yelled at their friend for misbehaving. Was there anything I could have done to prevent this?

Not everyone loves animals and many children might be afraid of a pet. Introduce the dog to the guest at first, and if that doesn't work, remove the dog. My daughter's dachshund tends to bark and run after children, so I put her in another room to prevent any disaster ensuing.

WHY FAMILY
MATTERS

"Life is not so short but that there
is always time for courtesy."

— RALPH WALDO EMERSON

Before I became a mother, I was so lucky to have had a strong and happy relationship with my sisters, parents, and grandparents. During my childhood, being with our extended family was a little challenging, given the fact that we were living so far away in Hong Kong, but my parents invited our grandparents to visit every other year, and every summer we would go to stay with them in Cape Cod and Boston. Although we saw each other only once or twice a year, my grandmother always sent me birthday cards and notes for other occasions, which I still have in a folder my mother put together for me. Growing up, I saw how important family ties were, and I am trying to instill this same awareness in my children. I feel that having a solid relationship with my parents and in-laws strengthens our family circle and teaches children the blessings of family.

In one of my blog posts, I wrote about the importance of grandparents. If your parents are healthy and able to take part in your life, they can play a positive role in your child's development. In my post, I addressed the fact that some grandparents tend to be more lenient when it comes to rules and may occasionally go against how we choose to parent. At times like these, it's important to mind your manners and find a polite way to broach the topic; just because they are close family members doesn't mean they shouldn't be afforded the same level of courtesy you would extend toward anyone else. Family issues should be addressed with politeness.

Every family has its own dynamic, and you can't stop your children from arguing with one another. It's normal and healthy, and teaches them how to manage their way through their own emotions. But when you become a parent, it's important to work toward creating good relationships with family members regardless of familial quirks. In certain circumstances, this can be hard, but you can make it easier by trying to keep children out of family arguments and issues. This is especially difficult when wounds are still raw and emotions are running high; it requires being accepting and nurturing, and keeping conversations about a family member you aren't on good terms with away from the ears of any children.

As children mature, they will naturally develop their own relationships with relatives; my children are so close with some of their cousins, and a few of them have become true friends. But we all hear heartbreaking stories of families that don't talk any more, and I firmly believe in doing all that is possible to avoid such an outcome. I'm not here to lecture you on how to keep your family together. But, as a mother of five, I'd love to share some of my suggestions on how we can be courteous and respectful to one another—because, after all, family matters.

House Rules

Here are some house rules that we follow to make sure we are kind to one another when we're at home or traveling.

Family time

This might seem like a no-brainer, but in our overworked and multi-scheduled world it's vital to carve out time spent as a family. This means trying your best to make it quality time rather than a chore. It could be a holiday together, or a weekend or day a month dedicated to a grandmother or mother-in-law. You could play a board game, cook a meal together, or perhaps go to the theater. Make it creative and maybe intervene if you find that a grandparent or another family member doesn't know quite how involved they should be.

We used to have a family game night, but I've since replaced this tradition with a puzzle table. I've noticed how this is a great way to collaborate, bond with your family, and learn to share. However, I'm still a fan of a game night, or a family night in general, as any activity during it presents an opportunity to reinforce good manners. A child can learn a lot from waiting their turn or sitting quietly with a grandparent. Being polite and considerate could involve something as simple as thinking of others when choosing a film for the family to watch. When you have young children, it truly feels as though they will be little forever, but this isn't the case and they grow up fast. Making time for your children and establishing space for fun family activities is how we create family memories and rituals. I am a great believer that family rituals deepen relationships.

Family calendar

When I was little, I remember my grandmother keeping a calendar where she wrote down all of her family members' birthdays and any special occasions. As mentioned earlier, she always sent me birthday cards, which arrived promptly on the day. It made me feel special, and it also showed me that she cared. I myself have a large family, and—inspired by my grandmother—have now created my own calendar. (Unlike my grandmother's, however, mine is digital.) When you come from a big family, it can be hard to keep track of everyone. Noting down birthdays and other important dates ensures that you won't offend anyone by missing their significant day. A card, gift, or even just a phone call shows that you haven't forgotten and will help to make it a special day for the recipient. Remind children that they don't need to give (or receive) a lavish present for every birthday or milestone; it really is the thought that counts.

Family group chat

In addition to having a family calendar, we all keep in touch digitally
with a designated family group chat, as touched on in Chapter 2. When
children are young, parents having a chat forum with close family
members can be a godsend, as it makes it easy to reach out during this
period of new parenting when you're perpetually strapped for time.

Now that my children are older, we use the group chat to send each
other funny articles and also update one other on various events
we want other family members to be a part of. It's a fun and
casual way of staying in touch with everyone and of keeping
up with what's going on in other family members' lives. Be
mindful of how much you text and don't be a braggart and
boast about grades and achievements.

Be nice!

It's hard not to fight with the people closest to you.
The first person most of us learn how to argue with is usually
a sibling. While I wouldn't want to raise a child who never speaks up,
I do want my children to be able to express what they want without
intentionally upsetting their siblings with hurtful words. Remember:
words can sting, and the impact they make can be long-lasting.

Young children can be very demanding of their parents, and I have seen
plenty of parents give in to their tantrums. Keep in mind that you are
the parent, and you must learn to find a way to stop unruly behavior.
Don't be afraid to say that it's wrong; it will only get harder as they get
older. Set the rules and stick to them. Children entering their tween
years may often develop an attitude. Head this behavior off at the pass
by setting limits for your child, and explain that this isn't the proper way
to communicate.

Spending time with grandparents

Grandparents sometimes feel hesitant about making plans with their grandchildren because they don't want to appear intrusive, but this could mean that your children miss out on a wonderful, life-enhancing intergenerational connection. Finding a common bond between your children and their grandparents can be the answer. My mother and daughter, for instance, both have a love of fashion, art, and design, and will often go to galleries and shows together. If you notice that your parents or in-laws are having a hard time engaging with your children, gently suggest activities they might both like to do together, as you know your child best.

Grandparent etiquette

When it comes to spending time with grandparents,
children should keep the following rules in mind.

Look smart An outing with grandparents is the perfect
opportunity to teach your child the importance of dressing
up. Seeing that an effort has been made for them will be
greatly appreciated by most grandparents.

Be considerate Children need to be mindful of generational
differences. A grandparent might not want to watch your
child play video games, for example, or go to see a loud movie with them.
Suggest they spend this time at a museum or the theater, or doing another
activity that relates to a shared interest (see opposite), instead.

Mind your p's and q's Teach your child to be extra polite to their
grandparents; being mindful of their manners really will go a long way.
(Note: good manners should be extended toward all elders, family or not!)

Set out the house rules Parents should have an honest and open
conversation with the grandparents to explain the house rules. This works
both ways: if your parents and in-laws have their own set of rules about
expectations, whatever they may be, discuss them—and if your child is old
enough, go over these standards with them. You are entrusting your parents
with your child and must accept that they might not share the same beliefs
as you. Remember: they are parents too, so be kind.

Make it personal Written thank-you cards and homemade
art projects are always welcomed by grandparents. Keeping
the communication channels open will help your kids'
grandparents to feel more involved in their grandchildren's
early years. It's also important for children to learn the
value of having an older relative in their life.

*Family can bring out the best and the worst in us,
so here are a few etiquette tips to help families
communicate mindfully.*

Elderly relatives

It can be hard to get a toddler to calm down or keep their voice down, but do your best to make sure your children are well-mannered and respectful around elderly relatives. Acting in a proper and gentle manner is particularly important if you are visiting an elderly relative in an assisted-living facility, so be sure to prepare your child beforehand about what is and isn't appropriate behavior, especially since young children might find it hard to articulate if they are feeling uncomfortable. Kindness matters.

Cousins and similarly aged relatives

As I mentioned at the start of the chapter, there is nothing sweeter than seeing cousins who get along. However, just because your children are related, it doesn't mean they actually have anything in common. As the saying goes, you can't choose your family—but you can try to make the effort. If your child doesn't want to hang out with their cousins, ask them why. Explain why it's important for them to get to know their cousins or other family members, and what the value is in trying to find a common denominator. You shouldn't force cousins to be best friends, of course, but do encourage them to develop their own relationships with their family. A little effort will go a long way.

"Oh, you like to rollerskate too?"

Blended and divorced families

This is a delicate subject and every situation is unique. If you have
a blended family or are from a divorced family, it's vital to teach your
children to be respectful to any new family members. It can be hard for
a parent to see an ex at a school event or to spend a holiday alone without
their children—remember, this isn't easy for anyone involved—so try to
come up with a regular holiday schedule or discuss who will be attending
which school or sports event. Plan well, so you and your child are never
surprised. Communication is key, and I truly believe that manners are
crucial here. At the end of the day, it's your child who shares the family
member. Your child will care deeply—and equally—so don't lose sight
of how your child feels. When discussing planning, be sure to keep your
child well away from any drama.

One of the positive sides to a blended family is that the family grows and there are more people to care about your kids—and also for your kids to care about. I have many friends who have exceptional relationships with their step-siblings, and I have witnessed ex-members of families spending a great deal of quality time together as a family. The key is to be forward-looking and do your best to make it a smooth transition.

Godparents

It is an honor to be asked to be someone's godparent. Not everyone understands exactly what this entails, however, and some people may be apprehensive of taking on the mantle. (I have been asked many times if it is considered rude to decline, if invited to be a baby's godparent; in some cultures it is considered not only rude but also a social faux pas!) If, for some reason, you can't accept this privilege, sit down and have a face-to-face chat with the expectant or new parent, letting them know firstly how honored and touched you are and then explaining the reasons why you have to decline.

If you are asked to be a godparent and you accept, you should play an active role in the child's life. Although historically a godparent's role involved being responsible for the child's religious education, these days many godparents are not chosen for any form of religious affiliation at all. Rather, being a godparent is a sign that you are considered a close member of the family. Responsibilities include making sure you are aware of special dates and, of course, spending some time with your godchild. So be sure to add any relevant dates to your calendar!

Choosing a godparent

When deciding on godparents, choose thoughtfully. Pick someone who has a meaningful relationship with your family. When my husband and I were choosing godparents we thought about cousins and family members first, but also we picked good friends who we felt would always have our children's best interests at heart and who would foster a good relationship with them.

Keep it in the family

Family members will inevitably share stories and feelings with one another that are extremely personal. These are the things that bind us. Young children, however, may not be aware that something they have overheard should not be repeated outside the family, so explain early on that it's not nice to share others' secrets. You will hopefully avoid private matters accidentally being repeated to your children's friends or even their friends' parents.

Siblings may try to use secrets as currency to attempt to control one another. This type of behavior should be nipped in the bud! If such a situation arises, boundaries must be established. Explain to siblings that they shouldn't read one another's texts or open doors without first knocking. Setting rules about how to show consideration for other family members' privacy will help everyone to get along better—and establishing these rules early on also makes it easier for children to accept them as the norm, especially since respecting boundaries will be such an integral part of their adult life.

YES

NO

Long-distance family relationships

As someone who grew up abroad and also lived abroad as an adult, I have firsthand experience in keeping extended family close when they are spread out across the globe. Here are some tips:

Set up a weekly video-chat date, using Zoom or FaceTime, for example. This ritual should be firmly set in your family's calendar. Sundays are always a good choice for calling Grandma/Grandpa.

Try to create a nice space for relatives when they come to visit. If you don't have room, find a welcoming place nearby where they can stay.

Be aware of the time difference when texting and reaching out.

Keep a private blog, photo album, or private social media account to share with other family members about time spent in other cities, and encourage other family members to do the same. It's a great way to keep up with everyone.

Try to meet halfway or come up with a compromise if it's tricky to visit. I know many families who feel they must travel together, but sometimes it can be easier for one parent to take one child back home for a visit. It isn't bad etiquette to travel without your spouse, even if you might get a few looks from older relatives. I often travel with one child and will make it a special trip between us.

Top Tips

My good friend always refers to herself as my child's aunt. I don't feel comfortable with this—how do I broach the topic?

This happens quite a lot. In fact, when I was growing up, I was used to calling family friends "Auntie" (although, I grew up in Asia, where it's the norm for children to address close family friends that way). If you don't like it, simply be polite and say that you prefer to reserve that title for your child's relatives. Your friend will understand if mentioned with kindness.

My ex-husband's wife has been showing up at school events with him. I appreciate that she cares about my child, but I don't want her there. Can I ask my ex not to bring her?

It really depends on whether or not it makes your child uncomfortable; after all, your child may be uneasy just because you are. At the end of the day, remind yourself that it's about what is best for your child.

I host every family event at my house, and none of my relatives ever offer to host instead. I'm afraid that if I don't do it, the family won't spend time together. What should I do?

Communication is always key in fostering good family relationships. There might be a reason behind all of this—maybe your in-laws are afraid to host because they think you'll get upset, for instance. Always ask before assuming.

My mother-in-law lives abroad and can only travel once a year due to the cost. She stays for six weeks, which I find too long, but my husband says she likes to spend time with the family. How can I raise the issue without offending her?

Work toward a compromise. Suggest that six weeks may start to infringe on your relationship with her, and in order to keep things on good terms, two to three weeks might work better.

Should I bring my child to my uncle's funeral?

It really depends on how your child would feel. In certain cultures it's seen as part of normal family interaction. I would, however, make sure your child understands what it is they are attending.

NAVIGATING HOLIDAY CELEBRATIONS

"The hardest job kids face today is
learning good manners without seeing any."

— FRED ASTAIRE

Ever since I was a little girl, the two weeks leading up to Christmas have always been the most exciting time for me. Decorating the tree, listening to Christmas music on the playlist, being at home, the pervading scent of pine coupled with the aroma of a holiday candle, the seasonal sprigs of holly … such a festive lead-up to this wonderful time of year. Although Christmas is a Christian holiday, regardless of your religion, the holidays should be in the spirit of family. I love embracing holidays, and I put in as much effort for Halloween as I do for Thanksgiving—and I am known to decorate madly!

In addition to decorating, I love to have holiday-themed treats around the house for my children or any guests who come to visit during the holiday period. This could be anything from little chocolate hearts placed on the breakfast table on Valentine's Day to themed dinners and fortune cookies for Chinese New Year. During the winter season, I'll set up a hot chocolate station, complete with jars of marshmallows and also tins of peppermint bark. Now that my children are older, we still enjoy family traditions like decorating the tree and baking together. We've made gingerbread men, pies for Thanksgiving, and dyed and painted Easter eggs. We even have family holiday playlists that we share, to put us all in the holiday mood.

Holidays are about being with family and friends. From Hanukkah to the Fourth of July, it's never bad manners to go over the top; to celebrate and have a good time. We can also take the opportunity to teach the little ones good behavior during family celebrations.

House Rules

Here are the family rules we follow during the holiday season to help remind us of what's important and to be mindful of how we treat one another.

Hosting

When hosting an event, I try to involve my children. I ask them to help with the decorations or food preparation or even menus. It's a way of teaching a child to take part in the act of hosting in formal settings and of getting them used to the idea of grown-up parties and how to behave around adults. Don't forget, however, that when your children are involved, they will be watching you, so you need to be aware of your behavior. When my children were younger, on occasions when I felt it was appropriate, I'd let them sit with us at one of our house dinners. I'd also set up a small children's table if they had friends who were staying for dinner. I always reminded them to be extra thoughtful about their manners at these gatherings, as they had been allowed to eat with the adults.

Being a guest

Being a guest is an honor that someone has bestowed upon you. That might sound a bit pretentious, but if you think of it that way, it will make you be a better guest. If someone has invited you to their home for a party or for the weekend, you must try to be respectful and courteous. Learn what their house rules are and follow them. There is nothing more gratifying than inviting a friend or family member for a weekend who turns out to be polite, respectful, and well-mannered. For instance, if their children have an earlier bedtime, you might want to modify your child's. Remind your children to clean up after themselves as it's not the host's responsibility.

Formal dinner party etiquette

When my children were a bit older and were able to sit with the adults while we were living in the UK, we were often invited to formal weekends away. Before attending, I had to teach my kids about the rules that are observed at formal English dinner parties.

Unlike at casual events, at a formal dinner, you can't just talk to the person seated across from you. During the first course, it is traditional for women to talk to the person seated to their left (which generally means that the male guests will be talking to the person to their right). After the first course, you turn to talk to the person on the other side (the "turning of the table"), and at dessert, you revert back to the first side, but this time it's a little more relaxed and you can talk both ways. This might sound a bit stuffy, but the concept was created so that everyone has the chance to speak and no one is ever left out.

Whenever we visited friends, I always reminded my children beforehand to mind their table manners and to be thankful to the host and to the family. They had to remember to ask permission for something, whether it be to watch a movie, play outdoors, or even eat a cookie or snack. Teach your child that it is bad manners to refuse to eat what is served for lunch or dinner. It is also considered rude to ask for a personalized dietary menu unless your child has a severe food allergy or intolerance.

Holiday cards

Posing for a holiday card isn't at the top of any child's list of things to do, and every year I find it gets harder and harder to get my kids to smile for a family portrait. In a culture of selfie-addicted children, it's ironic that so many of them complain when asked to participate in a simple family photo! Many families send cards with photos from vacations, but if you are the type of family that enjoys taking an annual portrait, sit down and chat with your kids about the importance of doing something that is meaningful to other members of the family. I always told my children that they would cherish these reminders of their childhood when they grew up, because once children become young adults, so often I've noticed their replacement by the family pet in cards sent to me by friends. I also showed my children old photos of my family from my childhood. It's photos like these, and the accompanying stories, that teach children the importance of family history.

Once your holiday cards are ready to go, be sure to sign them! If you can't sign all of them, at least try to sign the ones you're sending to family members and close friends, as it can appear thoughtless if you don't. A little effort goes a long way and, since many people display (and sometimes keep) holiday cards, it's nice to see that someone has signed the card for that extra personal touch. In addition, if your child is old enough, ask them to sign the cards as well.

Signature style

In recent years, cursive writing has crept out of the elementary-school curriculum. Children learn to write in print, and as they get older, they spend more time learning how to type. Due to this shift, children of the newer generation often don't have a signature.

Many children can't sign their passports, library cards, school IDs or forms, or other official documents when required to do so. If your child doesn't know how to write in cursive, you might want to get them to practice writing a signature at home.

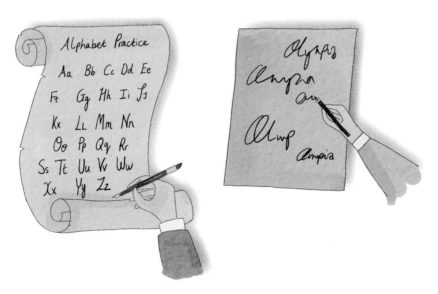

A signature not only serves as a proof of identity—it's also a great way to showcase self-expression. This is something they will use for their lifetime. If they're reluctant to learn, remind them that a signature is an autograph, and that most celebrities, presidents, and important figureheads have a notable one.

1. Something They Want

2. Something They Need

3. Something To Wear

4. Something To Read

Gift giving

You don't have to spend your entire life savings on buying presents. In fact, there is something to be said for smaller, more understated gifts that are thoughtfully chosen. Younger children aren't able to earn their own money, and holidays and birthdays are often the only opportunity they have to get certain toys and items that parents wouldn't normally purchase at other times of the year. Children shouldn't be greedy, however, and should always be grateful if they have received a new toy. If a relative gives your child a gift they don't like, make sure your child knows to acknowledge the gift positively (remember the party-gift etiquette we looked at in Chapter 6) and also sends a thank-you note.

I read about a great way to purchase a present: it's called the Four Gift Rule. This premise offers great guidance, especially as my kids get older and buying presents is more challenging. The idea is to simplify presents into four categories: Something you know they want, something they need, something to wear, or something to read.

As a parent, I remember how disappointed little ones can get if they ever feel left out. So, during the holiday season, it's a good idea to have a few extra presents on hand for any unexpected visitors.

Large families

When you have a large family, the amount of shopping you have to do can be overwhelming. In addition to your immediate family, you might have a slew of cousins, aunts, uncles, and grandparents. To help alleviate  the hassle (and cost) of purchasing numerous gifts, some families opt to have a "Secret Santa," which entails purchasing a gift for one randomly assigned adult instead of buying gifts for everyone. Most families exclude children from the Secret Santa, so that each child receives gifts as usual.

However you decide to handle your holiday season, make sure it's discussed beforehand, so as not to offend an aunt, uncle, or any other relative who may be expecting a gift.

Giving back

The holiday season is the ideal time to teach your children about helping others, since it's the time of giving. Sometimes volunteering as a family is challenging because it's hard to find opportunities that allow younger children to join in. Many schools organize events when children are older; my children's school did harvest festival collection boxes and back-to-school backpack drives at appropriate times during the school year. When my daughter was little, she sang at a senior center with her school choir.

Giving back can be as simple as purchasing a toy or sorting through your coat closet to donate to a charity. At the end of the day, it's teaching your child to think of others and to help those in need.

THE BASICS

Following good holiday etiquette makes for
a happy holiday season.

Asking for an invitation adjustment

If you're invited to a party or get-together during the holiday season,
always check to see whether children are welcome. If they are but you feel
that your child might disturb others because of the timing of the event,
you might ask if you can still attend but limit the visit. For instance, if it
falls during your child's nap or bedtime, explain your situation to the host
and ask if you could stop by for dessert or coffee instead. It's never polite
to just show up late to a meal. It sounds simple, but communicating your
needs politely is the best form of etiquette. That said, don't go overboard
and expect the host to make too many concessions; after all, you don't want
them to be inconvenienced by having to accommodate your requests.

How to decline an invitation

If you can't attend a holiday invitation from a close friend or family member, a phone call is always a polite gesture. If you have received an invitation online, reply promptly and don't let it sit in your inbox; many of these invitations offer a "maybe" or "undecided" option, and this response is better than ignoring the invitation completely. Remember: when it comes to online invitations, the host will be able to see if you have viewed it and will wonder why you haven't responded if you don't send a reply.

Above all, be prompt and considerate in your response. Don't forget that the host has been gracious enough to invite you in the first place, so the least you can do is afford them the same courtesy in return.

Tipping/gifting

These days, most parents like to show their appreciation for teachers, nannies, or other caregivers in their children's lives by giving them a bonus or gift in the holiday season. Be sure to check first, however, if there are any regulations you need to abide by; if you want to give a present to your child's exceptional preschool teacher, for example, find out the school's rules on gifting. If there is a no-gifting policy, then a nice handwritten card or a

family holiday card with a signature will suffice. (When there is a no-gifting policy, a class parent will often reach out for donations toward a class gift for the teacher.)

If you employ a nanny, a good rule of thumb is to give them two weeks' pay as a holiday bonus. Or, if you have a regular babysitter who comes one night a week, say, a small token such as a gift card is always well received.

What to bring the host

Most events you are invited to as a family are personal occasions, and in those situations, it's polite to ask if you should bring something. If you are a weekend guest for a holiday celebration, you could take a scented candle, a book, a board game, some homemade biscuits, or a nice box of chocolates, for example. Be creative and show that you've put some effort into choosing—or making—the gift.

Once you arrive, remind your children to keep their rooms as tidy as possible. Also, if you're staying for a long weekend, an offer to take the host out for dinner will always be greatly appreciated.

What to pack

The holidays are a time for travel, and you want to be sure to pack appropriate clothes and other items if you're staying with family or friends. If you are visiting someone, find out what's on the agenda. If they expect their guests to wear formal clothes for the holiday meal, it's best to be prepared. It's always better to ask so you don't find yourself hiking up a mountain in heels or turning up to a black-tie dinner in a pair of blue jeans.

TOP TIPS

My sister always wants to bring her dog and says her kids would be heartbroken without him. Last time, he chewed all of my son's toys. Is there a polite way to say don't bring him?

As an animal lover, I understand how hard it is to leave your dog at home when visiting relatives or friends, but I would never even consider taking one of my dogs to someone's house. It isn't impolite to say no. You don't have to go into a lengthy explanation—just say it's your house rule.

Last year, we received holiday cards from my children's friend's parents. Do we have to send cards in return?

It's polite to reciprocate; I usually just send new cards to my children's class. Remember: holiday cards are a courteous way of acknowledging and sending warm wishes not only to friends and family we care about but also to people who have made a contribution to our lives, like doctors, co-workers, and so on.

We live abroad and usually come back home for the winter holidays. This year we want to host, but our families say the trip is too long. Should we be offended?

If you live abroad, you have to accept that family won't always be able to visit. Try to make plans well in advance so no one gets any last-minute surprises. If you live far away, give family members plenty of time to make the choice to come to visit and to plan their schedules.

My cousin has four young children and it's hard to manage when we invite her whole family to a gathering. Is it rude to invite her without the kids?

If you've had your cousin and her children at your family gatherings in the past, then be honest with her and politely mention that you need some adult time without any children. It doesn't mean that you won't have them all over again. You're establishing healthy boundaries, which is important.

I have an uncle who never knows when it's time to leave. How do I get him to go without hurting his feelings?

This is fairly simple. All you have to do is to tell him you are tired and the party is over. He shouldn't get offended if said in the right tone.

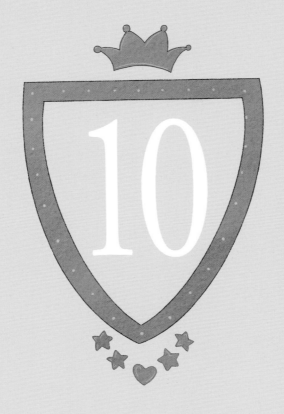

BABY ETIQUETTE

"Children have never been very good at listening to their elders,
but they have never failed to imitate them."

— JAMES BALDWIN

Congratulations! There is no way to describe the feeling of meeting your baby for the very first time. After having five children—a daughter and four sons—I can honestly say that the joy never diminishes. Even though it's been a few years since I've had to change a diaper, I'm still keyed into the world of parenting. In 2000, I founded a designer baby and childrenswear brand, Marie-Chantal. When designing a new collection, I tend to base my styles around memories of my childhood and those I have of my children. This is also how I shaped my role as a mother. My own mother taught me how to be appreciative and tactful; she would always send the perfect gift, say the right words, and put a lot of effort into helping others. So, I would like to share with you here some of the invaluable advice I've picked up from her, and from my own experience over the years, to help make the prospect of new parenthood a little less daunting.

There are a number of books explaining what to expect when you become a parent for the first time, but most of them don't cover the etiquette surrounding pregnancy and becoming a new mother or father, or even offer guidance on how to behave around babies. In our digital age, where an email with a photograph of the baby or a social media post serves as an announcement, new rules are being established all the time. Are you responsible for sending a gift, for instance, if you happen to be one of the recipients of an email announcement, or does a simple congratulatory reply suffice? And what should you take to a gender-reveal party?

The answer is the same for both: you aren't required to give gifts to either the sender of the email or the person who throws the party. If those answers surprise you, you're not alone. I often break these rules of etiquette, however, and consider it polite to send or bring a small token to show that you are thinking of your friend at this special time. Luckily, though, you won't end up in the doghouse if you didn't pick up a present.

House Rules

At the time of writing, it's been over a decade since I was the mother of a baby, and there have been so many new concepts in the parenting world since then, from the current trend of "sip and see" parties to dedicated Instagram pages for babies.

Now that my children are older, the tables have turned, and I am the person who attends new-baby celebrations, rather than having them thrown for me. From both old and new experiences, I have curated a list of house rules to follow.

Don't touch

When I was pregnant, people loved to reach out and touch my belly, often without even asking me if it was okay. If someone had done that when I wasn't pregnant, it could have been seen as harassment, yet the minute you start growing a bump, people feel that it's somehow allowed. Touching a pregnant woman's belly—or even asking to touch it—is a definite etiquette no-no, because it puts the woman in an uncomfortable position.

Don't comment

Just as you should keep your hands to yourself, it's best to keep your comments to yourself too. Don't be tempted to try to predict the baby's gender by the way the mother carries. And refrain from asking her if she's in her ninth month or if she's having twins. It's absolutely fine, however, to ask when she's due—just be polite in response to her answers. I wouldn't tell a pregnant mother horror stories of your endless sleepless nights with a newborn, for instance! If you say anything, it should be positive and loving. I feel it's always best to be a good listener and, if asked questions, to keep your responses upbeat and nurturing.

When a friend reaches out to you for advice, let them know you are there for them, but watch what you say. Nobody is truly prepared for being a first-time (or even second-time!) parent, so let them have their own experience and try not to overload them with your stories. Be supportive, not a know-it-all, and realize that parenting has been going on since the dawn of time, and you're only one parent.

Taking your child to visit a baby

If you are visiting your friend and would like to take your child along, it's courteous to ask if you can bring them—don't assume they are invited. Some new parents are wary of children visiting, and you should respect their wishes. If your child has a sniffle or a lingering cold, leave them at home; the last thing you want to do is bring a sick child into a house with a newborn. Children may sometimes be harboring germs before they show any symptoms, so they should keep their distance from the baby regardless and follow the new mother's lead.

Children do love babies, so if you do take your child along, make sure they don't overwhelm the newborn. My rule would be to let them touch only their little feet, and to try to keep them away from the baby's face.

Respect the parent's wishes

When a friend has a baby, make plans to see the newborn, but on the new parent's terms. In short, be sensitive to the parent's needs. If they want to wait a period of time before people meet their baby, please be understanding. Keep your first visits brief and try not to overstay your welcome. Don't be offended if your friend is overwhelmed and unable to make plans; this is a joyous yet transitional period in a person's life, and some people want to have the first month to themselves to bond with their baby. You need to be there for your friend, but make it about them and not about yourself. Let them know you are thinking of them by sending some celebratory flowers.

Hosting hiatus!

If you are the one with the new baby, you don't have to be the perfect host. This is one period of your life when you can relax your hosting skills! When visiting a new parent, I usually take them gifts and chocolates, and I really wouldn't want—or expect—them to do anything for me while I'm there.

The minute you become pregnant you'll quickly learn the art of multitasking. From shower planning to figuring out how to organize all your prenatal appointments while navigating a tricky work schedule, it's a busy but magical time in your life.

Here are a few planning pointers for before and after the big date.

Announcement

Traditionally, pregnancies are announced after twelve weeks. Once the baby is born, etiquette states that you have up to six months to send out a birth announcement, but in this tech-savvy world, people often post announcements on social media within an hour of delivery! Even if you send an email or post the news online, I still think it's nice to send a formal paper announcement with a photograph, as it's such a lovely keepsake for your baby when they are older and want to look through their baby books. If you want to go down this road, you will have to collect everyone's home addresses. (I know—the hassle! But it's actually quite an enjoyable process.) Remember that you have up to six months to do it, so wait until you feel settled and ready.

If you are on the receiving end of a formal announcement, the general rule of thumb is to send a gift, even if you went to the baby shower or plan to visit to say hello. I like to send flowers a week or two after the baby is born or send a small gift with a handwritten card.

Constantine Alexios

29th October 1995

Parties

There are so many ways to introduce your baby to the world—it's entirely down to personal preference. If you have a baby shower, you will most likely not be throwing this event for yourself; it is traditionally hosted by a close friend or sibling (so be sure to thank them with flowers on the day of the shower). A baby shower should be held about a month before the due date. Alternatively, if it's your second child, a friend might want to throw you a "sprinkle." A sprinkle is essentially a baby shower on a much smaller scale, and it is usually held when there is an age gap between children.

If you're superstitious and the idea of a baby shower doesn't appeal to you, try planning a "sip and see" instead. A Southern US tradition, this is an informal event where people drop by to "see" the baby. It is usually held around two months after the baby is born or home from the hospital.

Appropriate gifts

Don't know what to give? Here are some
thoughtful ideas for a variety of events.

Baby shower It's advisable to select a gift from the registry, as most new parents will have wish lists and you will be able to buy them what they really need. One option is to get together with another friend and buy a larger joint gift, like a Moses basket or a pram. Failing that, you can never go wrong with any type of personalized baby gifts, a selection of onesies, a rattle, a baby blanket, or a toy for the nursery. Be creative.

Sprinkle Since a sprinkle is a shower for a second or third baby, most parents should already have the basics covered, so you can give a cute outfit or choose from one of the ideas mentioned above. You might also want to take a smaller gift for the older child so they don't feel left out.

Sip and see You are not required to bring a gift, but most people do, especially if the sip and see is the only party celebrating the new baby. Again, be creative and make sure the present is a thoughtful one.

Baptism/christening If you are a godparent and Christian, then you should offer to buy the baby's first cross. (In the Greek Orthodox and Russian Orthodox religion, one of the godparents will not only buy the baby's cross but will also offer to buy the baby's christening outfits, as there will be two to buy.) Alternatively, good godparent gift ideas can include a monogrammed baby item such as a blanket, a silver frame or feeding spoon, or a christening cup. If you are a guest at the service, you should also bring a gift.

Baby naming/bris Gifts are not usually taken to a bris or baby naming ceremony. If you wish, you could take a small present like an outfit for the baby, but it's certainly not required or expected.

Nursing

If you're able to nurse your baby, you might find yourself feeling self-conscious while nursing in public, at least initially. (Most people usually feel more confident once they've gotten used to doing it.) If you feel insecure about nursing while out and about, try doing it discreetly in a quiet area or use a nursing blanket. There are numerous articles about women being criticized for nursing in public—on planes or in restaurants, for example. The bottom line is that it is a woman's legal right to nurse in public, and you should never be made to feel uncomfortable for doing so.

There is no "bad etiquette" when it comes to nursing. The only time someone may be considered rude or deemed to have bad manners is if they judge a mother for not nursing or for the length of time the mother chooses to nurse. If you have strong opinions on how others should nurse or behave, please keep them to yourself.

Diapers

Changing a diaper is often one of those jobs that nobody wants to do. While there is no official etiquette surrounding diaper changing, there are some simple rules you should follow. For instance, if you're at a friend's house, don't just throw a changing pad down on their rug or decide where you're going to change your baby on your own. Be considerate and ask for the powder room or for another appropriate place to change a diaper.

Unsurprisingly, it's deemed disrespectful to change a diaper on any surface where someone will eat, so a restaurant booth is off limits. This may seem obvious, but I've seen it happen. Try to find a proper changing station or changing table, but if nothing is available and you're forced to improvise, do think of others and try to be neat and discreet.

Social media

Many people create Instagram accounts for their little ones. I'll admit, I love scrolling through pictures of babies, but new parents shouldn't spend more time trying to capture a moment for a post than enjoying their new baby in the present. Think about how your baby might react to this account when they are older. What if your parents had kept a log of every cute moment of your life for the world to see—how would you feel? You might be tempted to delete your baby's social media account after having thought seriously about that question. (I'm not suggesting you go that far, but do try to keep social media use in check.)

If you are posting pictures on your private social media page, avoid inundating friends or followers with a constant stream of images of your baby. The basic etiquette with regard to social media is to be respectful of your baby and others. My advice is to keep it cute and not overly curated.

TOP TIPS

My friend had a miscarriage—what is the appropriate
thing to say in these circumstances?

It really depends on whether your friend is crying out for help and needs
the support of a friend. Offer her as much comfort and compassion as she
needs. Be gentle and kind and help her through this difficult time.

A good friend asked if I would host her baby shower.
Won't her sister be offended? Also, if you host the shower,
does this mean you are obliged to pay?

If you are asked to host, you should offer to pay. However, if the guest list
starts to get out of hand, be frank and suggest that it might be best if a
few others help you with the event. Be a good sport and offer to host
with her sister.

Is it okay to invite guys to a baby shower?

I had my husband attend at the very end of my baby showers. It's perfectly
acceptable today to invite whomever you like to a baby shower.

My ex-husband's wife has had a new baby—my daughter's
sibling. Is it impolite not to send a gift?

Why not have your daughter give a gift if you're not comfortable sending
one? But if you happen to be on good terms, then by all means, send a gift.

People always want to touch my baby. How can I tell them
nicely that I'd rather they didn't?

A new baby is always such a treat to hold and touch, but it really should
be your decision, especially if the baby is very young and you are worried
about germs. Just explain politely that you'd rather they didn't. Don't be
a grump; be courteous and say no with a smile.

THE

FAMILY

NOTEBOOK

Date:

Family Contacts

MOTHER/
FATHER: _____   TEL: _____

BIRTHDAY: _____   YEAR BORN: _____

MOTHER/
FATHER: _____   TEL: _____

BIRTHDAY: _____   YEAR BORN: _____

GRANDMOTHER: _____   TEL: _____

BIRTHDAY: _____   YEAR BORN: _____

GRANDFATHER: _____   TEL: _____

BIRTHDAY: _____   YEAR BORN: _____

GRANDMOTHER: _____   TEL: _____

BIRTHDAY: _____   YEAR BORN: _____

GRANDFATHER: _____   TEL: _____

BIRTHDAY: _____   YEAR BORN: _____

School Contacts

SCHOOL: _____ PRINCIPAL: _____

ADDRESS: _____

TEL: _____ EMAIL: _____

TEACHER: _____ NURSE: _____

EVENTS & IMPORTANT DATES: _____

_____

_____

SCHOOL: _____ PRINCIPAL: _____

ADDRESS: _____

TEL: _____ EMAIL: _____

TEACHER: _____ NURSE: _____

EVENTS & IMPORTANT DATES: _____

_____

_____

SCHOOL: _____ PRINCIPAL: _____

ADDRESS: _____

TEL: _____ EMAIL: _____

TEACHER: _____ NURSE: _____

EVENTS & IMPORTANT DATES: _____

_____

_____

SCHOOL: _____ PRINCIPAL: _____

ADDRESS: _____

TEL: _____ EMAIL: _____

TEACHER: _____ NURSE: _____

EVENTS & IMPORTANT DATES: _____

_____

_____

Healthcare Contacts

FAMILY DOCTOR: ....

ADDRESS: ....

TEL: .... EMAIL: ....

IMPORTANT NUMBERS: ....

PEDIATRICIAN: ....

ADDRESS: ....

TEL: .... EMAIL: ....

IMPORTANT NUMBERS: ....

DENTIST: ....

ADDRESS: ....

TEL: .... EMAIL: ....

IMPORTANT NUMBERS: ....

VET: _____

ADDRESS: _____

TEL: _____ EMAIL: _____

IMPORTANT NUMBERS: _____

OTHER: _____

ADDRESS: _____

TEL: _____ EMAIL: _____

IMPORTANT NUMBERS: _____

OTHER: _____

ADDRESS: _____

TEL: _____ EMAIL: _____

IMPORTANT NUMBERS: _____

After-School Activities

CHILD: _____ ACTIVITY: _____

DAY: _____ TIME: _____

TEACHER/COACH: _____

ADDRESS: _____

TEL: _____ EMAIL: _____

SPORTS EQUIPMENT: _____

IMPORTANT DATES: _____

CHILD: _____ ACTIVITY: _____

DAY: _____ TIME: _____

TEACHER/COACH: _____

ADDRESS: _____

TEL: _____ EMAIL: _____

SPORTS EQUIPMENT: _____

IMPORTANT DATES: _____

CHILD: _____ ACTIVITY: _____

DAY: _____ TIME: _____

TEACHER/COACH: _____

ADDRESS: _____

TEL: _____ EMAIL: _____

SPORTS EQUIPMENT: _____

IMPORTANT DATES: _____

CHILD: _____ ACTIVITY: _____

DAY: _____ TIME: _____

TEACHER/COACH: _____

ADDRESS: _____

TEL: _____ EMAIL: _____

SPORTS EQUIPMENT: _____

IMPORTANT DATES: _____

Travel Tips

PACKING CHECKLIST

ITEM: .... ☐

ITEM: .... ☐

ITEM: .... ☐

ITEM: .... ☐

ITEM: .... ☐

ITEM: .... ☐

ITEM: .... ☐

ITEM: .... ☐

ITEM: .... ☐

ITEM: .... ☐

ITEM: .... ☐

ITEM: .... ☐

ITEM: .... ☐

ITEM: .... ☐

ITEM: .... ☐

Party Essentials

FAVORITE BAKERS

NAME: _____

ADDRESS: _____

TEL: _____ EMAIL: _____

NAME: _____

ADDRESS: _____

TEL: _____ EMAIL: _____

FAVORITE PARTY PLANNERS

NAME: _____

ADDRESS: _____

TEL: _____ EMAIL: _____

NAME: _____

ADDRESS: _____

TEL: _____ EMAIL: _____

To Wear or Not to Wear

CASHMERE & DELICATES: Handwashing items will care for them in the long term far better than using a machine. Always soak garments if they are soiled to loosen the dirt. Fill a clean sink with lukewarm water and pour in a gentle soap (I find baby shampoo the best!). Mix the water with your hand to create suds, then immerse the item and wash gently, taking care not to distort the garment shape. Rinse well in lukewarm (never boiling!) water, then gently squeeze (don't twist or wring, as this will cause damage) and roll the garment up in a towel to remove the excess moisture. Lay the garment out flat on towels to dry.

SHOES: Suede and nubuck shoes should be cleaned and waterproofed regularly. If they do get wet, stuff them with newspaper to help keep their shape, and allow them to dry slowly. Buy a good stiff brush and gently remove any mud once fully dry. For leather shoes, always remove shoelaces before you start to polish, to avoid staining. Creams or polish are best applied with a soft cloth; once dried, wipe off any excess with a clean cloth and buff to a beautiful shine using a natural bristle brush. Teach your child to get into the habit of cleaning their own shoes at an early age!

UNIFORM: School uniforms can be costly, so caring for items like blazers is a must. Wool blazers often smell stale if they get wet (akin to a wet pooch!), so be sure to hang in a warm place to dry, away from direct heat. For spillages or stains, use a damp sponge followed by a flick of a soft brush. Always use wooden hangers; wire hangers will cause the garment to become misshapen, especially when wet. Blazers should be professionally dry-cleaned every semester to ensure a long and happy school life! Dirty collars and cuffs respond well to a good thirty-minute soapy soak. For more stubborn stains, soak the garment in some vinegar or a solution of baking soda and water before your regular wash.

SPORTS EQUIPMENT: Don't let your kids leave their smelly sports clothes scrunched in a bag for days! Most modern sportswear is easily cared for and can go in a regular warm or cold machine cycle; any stains can be pre-treated before the wash. Football boots and sneakers should be allowed to dry naturally; you can then knock off the loose mud before cleaning with a damp cloth. (For white sneakers that have seen better days, try rubbing with some cream cleaner—good as new!)

CLOTHES SIZES

AGE	HEIGHT	CHEST	WAIST
0–3 m	62cm / 24½ in	–	–
3–6 m	69cm / 27¼ in	–	–
6–12 m	77cm / 30¼ in	49cm / 19¼ in	44cm / 17¼ in
12–18 m	83cm / 32¾ in	51cm / 20in	46cm / 18in
18–24 m	90cm / 35½ in	52cm / 20½ in	48cm / 19in
2–3 yrs	98cm / 38½ in	54cm / 21¼ in	50cm / 19¾ in
3–4 yrs	104cm / 41in	56cm / 22in	52cm / 20½ in
4–5 yrs	110cm / 43¼ in	58cm / 22¾ in	54cm / 21¼ in
5–6 yrs	116cm / 45¾ in	60cm / 23½ in	55cm / 21¾ in
7–8 yrs	128cm / 50½ in	64cm / 25¼ in	58cm / 22¾ in
9–10 yrs	140cm / 55in	69cm / 27¼ in	62cm / 24½ in
11–12 yrs	152cm / 59¾ in	75cm / 29½ in	67cm / 26½ in

SHOE SIZES

BABIES							
Europe	17	18	19	20	21	22	23	24
UK	1	2	3	4	5	5.5	6	7
USA	1.5	2.5	3.5	4.5	5.5	6	7	8
Japan	11.5	12	12.5	13	13.5	14	14.5	15

CHILDREN										
Europe	25	26	27	28	29	30	31	32	33	34	35
UK	7.5	8	9	10	11	11.5	12	13	1	1.5	2.5
USA	8.5	9.5	10	11	11.5	12.5	13	1	2	2.5	3.5
Japan	15.5	16	16.5	17	17.5	18	18.5	19	20	20.5	21.5

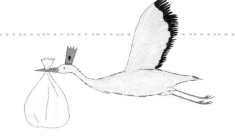

Baby Etiquette

IMPORTANT DATES

BABY SHOWER / SIP AND SEE: _____

LOCATION: _____ DATE: _____

BIRTH ANNOUNCEMENT: _____

DIGITAL ANNOUNCEMENT SENT: _____

POSTAL ANNOUNCEMENT SENT: _____

BABY'S FIRST FOOD

FOOD: _____ DATE: _____

BABY'S FIRST STEPS

LOCATION: _____ DATE: _____

BABY'S FIRST WORD

WORD: _____ DATE: _____

Epilogue

Although this book is a distillation of all I have learned as a parent of five (now-adult) children, here are some more detailed (and humorous) examples of some of the experiences I've had.

Dinner with the Queen

About a week before my wedding to my husband, Pavlos, I was asked to meet the Queen of England as we were getting married in London, and she had graciously accepted our invitation to attend with several members of her family. Her invitation to us was for dinner at Windsor; all went well, dinner was served, and by the time dessert was finished I was thankful to have made it through each course without breaking any rules of etiquette. However, the meal wasn't over.

At a formal dinner, normally coffee is offered at the very end, after the dessert. I was the first at the table to be served and watched as the coffee cup was placed in front of me. Then the butler bent down holding a silver tray with only cream and sugar. No coffee! I had never seen this before and I felt as if the entire table was watching to see what I would do, and I had to think quickly. At this point, I was blushing like mad and put up my hand politely, saying "No, thank you," passing on the cream and sugar in case it was a faux pas. I then watched in some confusion as several guests put the cream in their cup before the coffee. I found it strange, as I had always known to put the cream in after the coffee—as milk is taken after the tea has been poured.

Later, I gathered it was their custom. I hadn't made a mistake in not taking cream or sugar, as that is to my liking, but I learned something new. In the interests of the perennial debates about whether milk or cream come first or last, I've recounted this story to others and have heard various reasons for why one would put the cream and sugar in first. One of my friends told me that if you put cream or milk in first, before your tea, it will keep the china from staining, and others said that it prevents hot liquids from cracking what is, in those situations, very fine porcelain. Or maybe ... it is a little family in-joke.

Accidents do happen

What should you do if you break a glass or damage something when a guest under someone else's roof? Accidents do happen but a token or gesture of acknowledgment goes a long way. I had a friend who came to dinner with his partner; I didn't know the girlfriend well, but she tended to be quite animated and loud when talking. I had put out on the table some pretty glass bowls filled with chocolate. She picked one up and plonked it back on the table with a heavy hand and it smashed. She was so embarrassed but kept on turning the joke on me, which eventually became quite rude. She made fun of the fact that my bowls were so delicate, which made me feel awful. That said, a few days later she sent me a new bowl and apologized, which was the right thing to do.

Wait your turn

My daughter's friend had come to stay for the weekend with his girlfriend and we had organized a lovely lunch alfresco. We were a mixed group of my and my daughter's friends. Lunch was called; to my surprise, when I arrived my daughter's friend was already seated with a full plate in front of him and chomping away. I didn't say anything to offend my daughter. When I looked over at Olympia, she gave me a "Don't say anything" look. Yet, I remember being appalled at his bad manners. It's important to teach your children to respect the host's home and hospitality. I felt bad for my husband because he was the one grilling, and for a guest to eat before the host has finished at the barbecue or sat down himself is extremely disrespectful. It's important to emphasize the rule that someone else's home shouldn't be taken for granted.

Breakfast bagel

I once came down for breakfast on a weekend when my fourteen-year-old had a friend stay over. I was surprised to find my son's friend alone in our kitchen with all the pans out, butter sizzling and bacon about to be fried. He was making a bagel sandwich, and he had his entire setup going. I found it a bit odd that a guest was cooking in our home, and asked if I could help him prepare his breakfast. He said that he'd "got this," and happily carried on. Of course, I let him continue but I was surprised and baffled at how comfortable he was in my space. I felt bad about thinking his manners were rude, but was it okay to make your own breakfast in your host's house? I hoped he at least asked my son if it was okay. However, he should have asked an adult. Children should be taught that the way they behave in their home is one thing, but when they're a guest—no matter how comfortable they are with friends or relatives—it isn't their home. Teach your child to ask permission, and if they want to cook for themselves, to also offer to cook for the hosts—and more importantly, to clean up after themselves and their mess!

About the author

Marie-Chantal, Crown Princess of Greece, is the founder and creative director of Marie-Chantal, a leading international childrenswear brand, and the author of a popular parenting blog. Born in London, and one of three sisters, she spent her early years in Hong Kong before attending schools in Switzerland and Paris. Her passion and aptitude for art and design then led her to New York City, where she studied at the New York Academy of Art and New York University.

While many little girls dream of one day meeting their Prince Charming, for Marie-Chantal, the fairy tale came true! She married Pavlos, Crown Prince of Greece, in 1995, and they now have five children: Maria-Olympia, Constantine-Alexios, Achileas-Andreas, Odysseas-Kimon, and Aristide. Despite being immersed in the world of playdates and potty training, Marie-Chantal found a way to combine her two passions—being a parent and a designer—in the creation of her eponymous children's clothing line. The first collection was launched in 2000, the brand's ethos being nostalgia, timeless design, and a firm belief that children should look like children. The label has since gone from strength to strength, counting both royals and celebrities among its fans.

On writing a series of posts about etiquette in her parenting blog a few years ago, Marie-Chantal was surprised at how many people reached out to her asking for advice. Being a lifelong advocate of the importance of family and tradition and concerned that manners were being forgotten in our digital world, she realized there was a need for a guiding voice to help navigate today's social minefields—and so *Manners Begin at Breakfast* was born. With this indispensable handbook, Marie-Chantal hopes to take the stress out of modern parenting and help families learn and grow together. Manners begin at home, after all.

Visit her website at **mariechantal.com**

About the contributors

Dr. Perri Klass is a leading pediatrician and professor of journalism and pediatrics at New York University. She is also the national medical director of Reach Out and Read, a childhood literacy program in the US. Her most recent books are *The Best Medicine: How Science and Public Health Gave Children a Future*, and *Quirky Kids: Understanding and Supporting Your Child with Developmental Differences*, coauthored with Dr. Eileen Costello. A multi-award-winning author of books on parenting and medicine, Dr. Klass writes about children's issues for a wide range of publications. She has three children.

Visit her website at **perriklass.com**

Tory Burch is an award-winning fashion designer, businesswoman, and philanthropist. Launched in 2004, her eponymous American lifestyle brand is now a global empire, with more than 250 stores worldwide. In 2009, she set up the Tory Burch Foundation, to support women entrepreneurs. She lives in New York with her three sons.

Visit her website at **toryburch.com**

Nicholas Child is a Cheshire-based illustrator. His clients include Paperchase and Sainsbury's, and he has illustrated picture books for many publishers and authors. He enjoys illustrating in different mediums, with a love for watercolor and pencil. He has written his debut picture book—*The Wolf in Fancy Dress*, which teaches children the importance of being yourself.

Visit his website at **thechildrensillustrator.com**
or follow Nicholas on Instagram **@thechildrensillustrator**

Acknowledgments

A big thank you to my husband, Pavlos, for his love and constant support, no matter what I choose to do. Special thanks to my friends and family, especially my parents, who taught me from a young age that manners matter. To my close girlfriends, who encouraged me along the way and shared their tips. To my mother-in-law for her kind support in helping me with my questions on proper etiquette. To my children for keeping me humble, and for their love and support on this project. To Cimarron for her creative partnership. To Dr. Perri Klass and Tory Burch for their contributions to the project. To Nicholas for the utterly charming illustrations. To the Vendome family for their continued support, and to Alison for helping me to formulate my ideas. And, finally, to Bea for her constant encouragement and gentle push to keep me going.

Revised edition first published in 2024 by **The Vendome Press**
Vendome is a registered trademark of The Vendome Press, LLC
www.vendomepress.com

PALM BEACH
P.O. Box 566
Palm Beach
FL 33480

LONDON
Worlds End Studios
132–134 Lots Road
London, SW10 0RJ

PUBLISHERS Beatrice Vincenzini, Mark Magowan & Francesco Venturi
COPYRIGHT © 2024 Marie-Chantal of Greece

Distributed worldwide by Abrams Books

ISBN: 978-0-86565-446-4

CREATIVE CONSULTANT Cimarron Young
EDITOR Catharine Snow
PRODUCTION MANAGEMENT Mandy Mackie & Jim Spivey

Library of Congress Cataloging-in-Publication Data available upon request.

MIX
Paper | Supporting responsible forestry
FSC® C016973
www.fsc.org

Printed and bound in China by
1010 Printing International Limited

First printing